YOUR KIDS: COOKING!

A recipe for turning ordinary kids into extraordinary cooks

BARBARA BRANDT, M.ED.

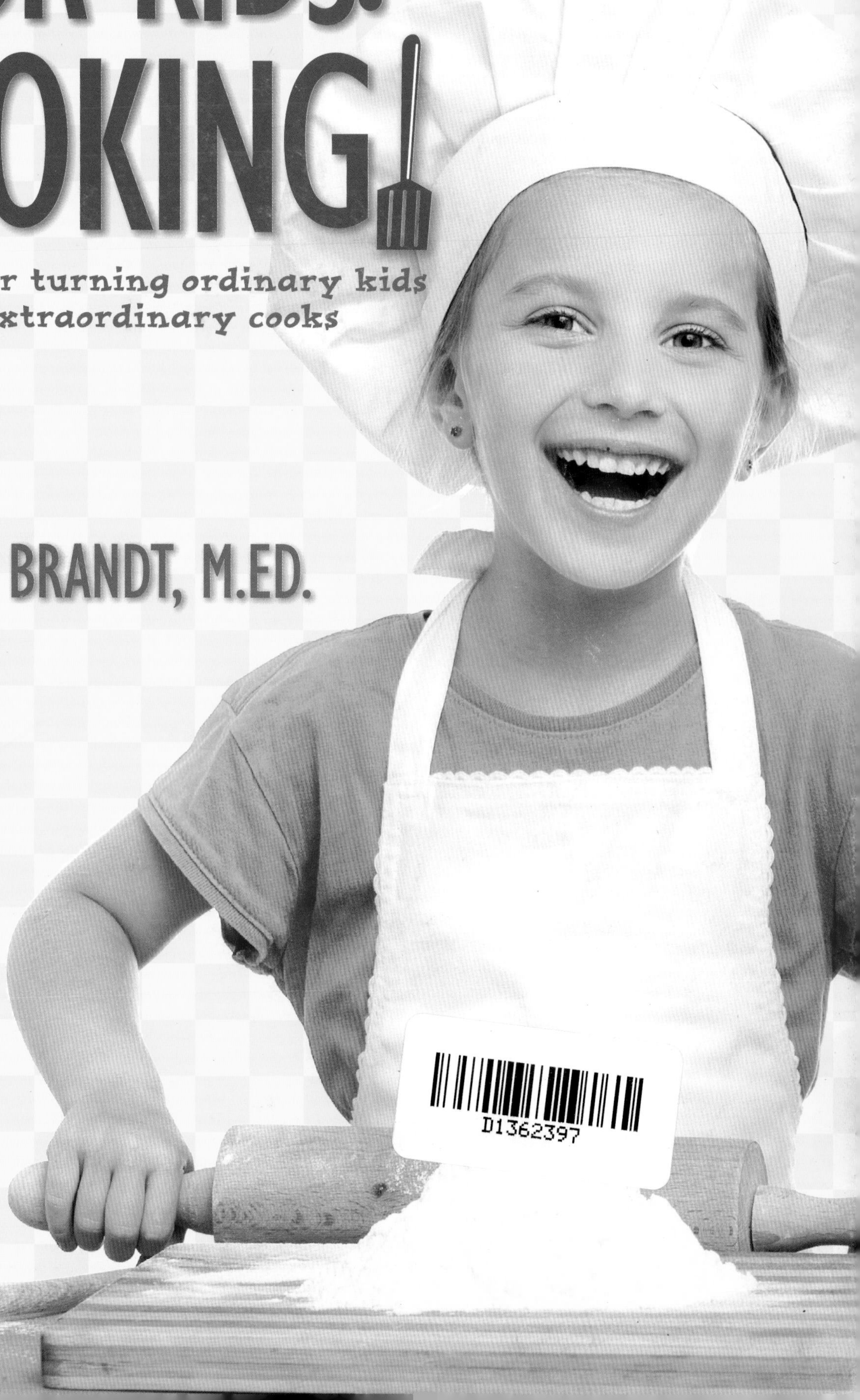

PUKKA PUBLISHING

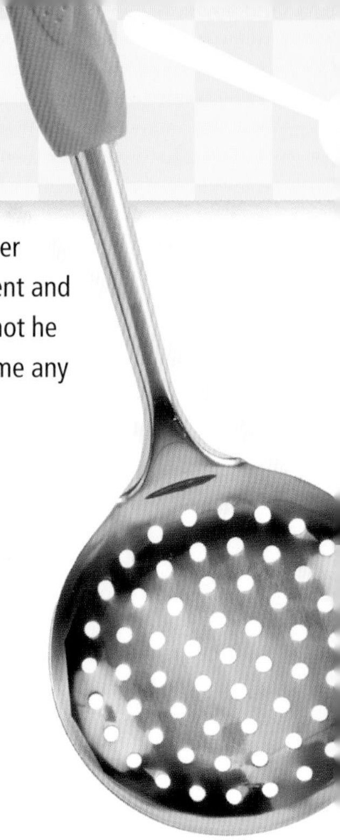

NOTE: This program is designed and intended to be used by children 8 years and up together with a supervising adult. It is assumed that the supervising adult will use their own judgment and common sense to determine how much supervision the young chef needs and whether or not he or she is capable of performing the skills taught. Neither the author nor the publisher assume any responsibility for any injuries or damages arising during the use of this program.

For Stella and Hunter and in honor my Grandma Gert—the greatest cook ever.

Editing	Elizabeth Sycamore
Managing Editor	Prowrite Consulting and Editing
Interior Design	rosa+wesley, inc.
Art Editor	Mekael Wesley-Rosa
Food Photography	Charles Raffety
Cover Design	rosa+wesley, inc.

A special thanks to Nicholas Jenkins, Sari Jones and Gladys Rosa-Mendoza who went above and beyond to bring my vision to reality.

PUKKA PUBLISHING

Published by Pukka Publishing, LLC
2434 Riata Road
Missoula, MT 59808

Printed in Malaysia

FIRST EDITION
ISBN: 978-0-9825952-1-3

Brandt, Barbara J.
Your kids : cooking! : a recipe for turning ordinary kids into extraordinary cooks / Barbara J. Brandt.
pages cm

ISBN: 978-0-9825952-1-3 (hardcover)
1. Cooking—Juvenile literature. 2. Food habits. 3. Cookbooks. I. Title.
TX652.5 .B73 2014
641.5123—dc23 2013920146

Table of Contents

SECTION I: Let's Get Acquainted!

SECTION 2: Let the Cooking Begin!

Let's Get Acquainted!

Preface

Teaching Kids to Cook: How Hard Can It Be?

My Failure

The old saying 'necessity is the mother of invention'—is typically true. But in my case, *Your Kids: Cooking!* was born out of failure—my failure at trying to teach my 11-year-old daughter how to cook. To my surprise and dismay, it wasn't quite as easy as I thought it would be.

Here I was, an experienced and accomplished teacher, a darn good cook, and a stay-at-home mom whose first priority has always been family. Though when it came time to teach my daughter how to cook, it was a complete disaster! Even though I knew how to both cook *and* teach, somehow trying to teach her to cook just wasn't working. Not only did she get bored as she sat there passively watching me show her how to do everything, I also mistakenly assumed that she had picked up on basic cooking techniques and terms from watching me cook over the years.

"Every failure brings with it the seed of an equivalent success."

– Napoleon Hill

For example, when we tried to make cookies, I assumed she knew the difference between a teaspoon and a tablespoon when measuring salt. I assumed she knew to set the dial on "bake," not "broil," when turning on the oven. Needless to say, we never got to taste our salty cookies because they came out of the oven looking like hockey pucks! The cookies ended up in the garbage and we both left the kitchen frustrated. Not exactly the "Normal Rockwell" mother-daughter moment I was hoping for. So much for teaching your kids to cook being fun!

Realizing that teaching my daughter to cook was going to require more than pulling out a recipe and hoping for the best, I started attending local cooking classes for kids to get some fresh ideas. I watched lots of kids sitting at tables—with no utensils or ingredients—and a chef in front of the class demonstrating how to prepare the recipe. A few of the lucky ones were invited up front to help out, but then only barely. For the most part the kids looked bored and unengaged—just like my daughter had been.

After learning all I could from the "experts," I made it my mission to create a method for parents to teach their kids to cook that would be fun and effective and keep kids engaged. One that would deliver what seemed to be the missing ingredient—*learning by doing!* The big question was how?

My Success

I'm not sure when it happened, but eventually it came to me—create a video with step-by-step demonstrations of how to make a recipe and combine it with written directions presented in a way that's easy for kids to follow. That way, kids could be shown how to prepare every step of the recipe and still be able to do everything themselves. The adult's role? Sous chef! There to help out when needed, provide encouragement, and keep things safe.

Well, guess what happened? The reversal of roles paired with a multimedia approach proved to be a success! My daughter learned to cook and loved every minute of it. I learned to "let go" and trust in her ability to do things on her own. And the two of us spent some much needed quality time together and had fun—learning, laughing, and growing closer. Mission accomplished!

My Gift to You and the Kids You Love

All the parents I know—moms and dads alike—agree that time spent with their kids is the most precious gift they can both give and receive. And to be able to spend that time teaching them a valuable lifelong skill, well, it just doesn't get much better than that.

Your Kids: Cooking! is my gift to you and the special young people in your life. And it is my most sincere wish that it brings the same kind of joy and fulfillment to you and your family that it has to mine.

Introduction

Why *Your Kids: Cooking!*

Did you ever wish you could count on your kids to have dinner on the table when everyone comes home hungry? Are you concerned about all the highly processed, nutritionally lacking convenience foods your kids eat? Would you like to squeeze some quality time with your child into your busy schedule, while at the same time teach them a valuable lifelong skill? If so, this copy of *Your Kids: Cooking!* is a gold mine! Here's why:

1 Your child will learn to cook . . . for themselves, for your family, and for the rest of their lives.

Much more than just a cookbook, YKC is a multimedia cooking program that teaches kids how to cook in a structured, fun, and engaging way. Through the seamless coordination of step-by-step demonstrations on the DVD with written and pictorial directions in the book, budding chefs are effortlessly guided through the preparation of 20 delicious and healthy meals the whole family can enjoy. Upon completing the program, young chefs will have acquired all the skills, techniques, knowledge and confidence they need to cook virtually anything they want.

2 Your child will be empowered to eat healthier.

In addition to learning to cook, kids also learn the basics of nutrition and how to make healthy food choices. Following the guidelines established by the USDA, young chefs learn about the five food groups that are the building blocks of a healthy diet, as well as which foods to eat more of and which foods to eat less of. The more kids understand about how to build a healthy plate, the easier it is for them to make healthy food choices—now, and for the rest of their lives.

3 You will spend quality time with your child.

Although kids do all the cooking themselves, the program is designed so you and your child can enjoy the experience together. In your role as "sous chef," you become your child's cheerleader and biggest fan—there to provide support and encouragement as your young "chef" takes on the challenge of learning to cook. And from time to time, when a little adult assistance is needed, you will be right there to provide help and keep things safe.

4 Success is guaranteed, whether you know how to cook or not.

You're not a cook, you say? No worries! Between the DVD and the book, kids receive all the direction and instruction they need to successfully complete each recipe on their own, regardless of your skill level or background. As sous chef, you will be there to provide help when needed and to keep things safe. Other than that, just sit back, relax, and enjoy the show!

5 Your child will develop self-esteem and confidence.

The multimedia approach used in the program makes it possible for kids to be 100% in charge of the entire meal preparation process. Taking on the challenge and responsibility for what is typically an adult role in the household is a surefire way to boost confidence and build self-esteem. Imagine your child beaming with pride and a sense of accomplishment as your family shares the meal he or she made all by themselves!

6 You'll create memories that will last a lifetime.

Laughing, talking, sharing, having fun! This is just some of what's in store for you and your child when you're in the kitchen together, enjoying each other's company. This program provides a unique opportunity for you and your child to build family traditions and create special moments you will cherish forever.

There is no greater gift parents can give their children than to spend time with them teaching them a valuable skill that will benefit them for the rest of their lives. Now you have everything you need to give them that gift.

Learning to cook is an adventure, and any successful adventure starts with a well-thought-out plan. You now hold that plan in your hands, so let the adventure begin!

Getting Started

Because YKC is a complete cooking *program*—as opposed to just a *cookbook*—it will be helpful to get acquainted with the nuts and bolts of how the program works. Before you dive in and start cooking, take a few minutes to review the following important information in the book and on the DVD.

In the book:

About the Program

A general overview of what's in store for you as you cook your way through the program.

Recipe-Lesson Sneak Peek

Guidelines for completing the recipe-lessons along with a sneak peek of all the important elements and features found on each page.

About the STACK

A complete list of all the skills, terms, and cooking know-how taught in each recipe-lesson.

Get Your Kitchen Ready!

A complete list of the equipment you'll need to make each recipe, along with suggestions for setting up your kitchen that will make recipe preparation easier.

Kitchen Safety

Important safety guidelines to review together to make sure the cooking experience is a safe one.

Note to the Sous Chef

Tips and suggestions for how to guide, support, and help the young chef from the sidelines.

On the DVD:

Welcome!

A brief introduction to the YKC cooking adventure.

How to Use the DVD

A short explanation of how the DVD and book are used together to complete a recipe-lesson.

Knife Safety

A quick demonstration on how to use a knife safely.

About the Program

Whisking, chopping, talking, laughing, and sharing . . . that's what's in store for you and your child as you embark upon this learning-to-cook adventure with YKC. Cooking with your child is a powerful way to instill a lifelong appreciation of good food and healthy eating habits. Children are naturally drawn to the challenge and creativity of preparing food—proudly sharing their culinary creations with family members and friends—making cooking a natural choice for fostering a sense of independence and competence as well as an awareness of the important role food plays in a healthy lifestyle.

Here's where YKC fits in. In just ten, easy-to-follow "recipe-lessons," young chefs will master over 100 cooking skills, techniques, and terms along with essential strategies that make meal preparation a snap. The recipes are carefully chosen and purposefully sequenced so that each recipe-lesson offers an engaging setting to learn new skills while continuously reviewing and reinforcing previously learned skills.

With an additional practice recipe in each recipe-lesson that reinforces target skills, and access to over 100 additional recipes on our website—all presented in YKC's unique and easy-to-follow format—this program empowers young chefs with all the knowledge and hands-on experience they need to cook anything they want!

Your Kids: Cooking! teaches kids to cook using three components:

- **A DVD** with complete, step-by-step demonstrations for each target recipe.
- **A book** with kid-friendly directions and pictures for each step.
- **A website** that provides additional support and resources to extend the learning beyond the book and the DVD.

Right from the start, YKC sets the scene for a positive, rewarding, and enjoyable shared-learning experience. Using recipes that appeal to kids and adults alike, budding chefs experience success and a sense of pride and accomplishment as they prepare delicious, wholesome meals the whole family will enjoy.

Here's how our integrated approach to teaching kids to cook makes that happen:

- **A multimedia format**—combining video, pictures, and print—creates a dynamic multi-sensory experience that supports all learning styles.
- **Complete step-by-step recipe demonstrations** on the DVD make it possible for any parent to successfully use the program with their child, regardless of their own cooking ability or experience.
- **A kid-friendly recipe format** with pictures and clear written directions makes every recipe easy for young chefs to follow all on their own.
- **Hands-on learning** with immediate real-world applications keeps kids engaged, enthusiastic and motivated to learn.
- **Putting kids 100% in charge** of the entire meal preparation process develops confidence, a sense of responsibility and self-esteem.
- **Working under the gentle guidance from a parent** (or other significant adult) promotes teamwork and cooperation.

Through this carefully planned learning experience, kids learn and grow in a variety of ways and enjoy every delicious moment as they prepare themselves for a lifetime of cooking wholesome, nutritious food.

The book and DVD are used simultaneously during the preparation of the target recipe. The seamless coordination between these two components provides a rich and powerful learning experience that is engaging and easy to use, guaranteeing success every step of the way.

YOUR KIDS: COOKING!
A recipe for turning ordinary kids into extraordinary cooks
Includes DVD with step-by-step demonstrations for making each recipe.
DVD
BARBARA BRANDT, M.ED.
YOUR KIDS: COOKING!

About the STACK

The complete set of **S**kills, **T**erms **A**nd **C**ooking **K**now-how kids learn in the program is called the STACK. Once the young chefs have "stacked up" all this knowledge, they will be

	Skills	Terms	And Cooking Know-how
French Toast	crack eggs whisk eggs use measuring spoons measure liquids flip food with a spatula	whisk dust flat spatula	preheating pans cooking with butter pan-frying
Macaroni & Cheese	grate cheese measure liquids measure dry ingredients	roux rubber spatula colander simmer full boil slow boil	cooking pasta kitchen safety *(draining pasta)* how to make a cheese sauce thickening sauces baking casseroles
Tamale Pie	chop onions brown ground beef use a knife safely open cans	brown chop bench scraper	browning meat kitchen safety *(using a knife)* cooking onions baking casseroles
Quiche	use a pastry blender roll out a pie crust	cutting in pastry blender rolling pin	making pie crust cooking bacon cooking spinach testing for doneness kitchen safety *(handling raw meat)*
Spaghetti & Meatballs	peel and mince garlic core tomatoes shape meatballs	mince dice	tomato-based sauces kitchen safety *(handling raw meat)* timing it right cooking garlic

ready to make virtually any recipe they choose. The chart below shows the new STACK items learned in each lesson.

	Skills	Terms	And Cooking Know-How
Stir-Fry	peel vegetables slice celery prepare peapods slice peppers	vegetable peeler slurry stir-fry wok	cooking with oil boiling rice best oils for stir-frying stir-frying basics Chinese spices
Eggs Benedict	separate eggs poach eggs chop herbs	poach separate eggs double-boiler	using a double-boiler making Hollandaise sauce poaching eggs
Chicken Parmesan	pound chicken bread chicken slice cheese	breading sauté	baking casseroles sautéing vegetables
Pork Chops	core and slice apples make a pan sauce	deglazing fond caramelization shallot	making a pan sauce boiling potatoes how to tell the doneness of meat
Pot Roast	mash potatoes sear meat	sear slow-cooking	searing meat slow-cooking

Recipe-Lesson Sneak Peek

The 20 recipes that make up the core of the YKC program are presented using an easy-to-follow, 14-page format called a "recipe-lesson." These recipes are specifically sequenced so that each one offers an engaging setting to learn new skills while continuously reviewing and reinforcing previously learned skills. For this reason, the recipe-lessons need to be completed in order to ensure that young chefs start with the basics and develop a solid foundation in fundamental cooking principles to build upon.

Here are guidelines for how to use the recipe-lessons so you can easily and effortlessly fit them into your family's normal meal preparation routine:

A day or more before you are ready to make a recipe:

Review the *Get Prepared!* section of the recipe-lesson. In this section you'll find important information to help you get prepared to make the recipe.

When you are in the kitchen and ready to start cooking:

Start the DVD. From the Recipe-Lesson menu, click on the recipe you are ready to make.

The hostess on the DVD will guide you the rest of the way, prompting you when it's time to follow the directions in the book.

A day or more after completing the recipe:

Make the *Test Your Skills!* recipe to practice and reinforce your new skills.

Whenever the mood strikes:

Make the *Reward Yourself!* recipe to reward yourself for a job well done!

For a complete and detailed explanation of the key features in each section of the recipe-lessons, review the remaining pages in this section.

Each recipe-lesson starts with a chapter opener that sets the stage for all the cooking fun that's in store for you.

LESSON 5

Spaghetti & Meatballs

SERVES: 4–6

COMPLETE THE LESSON: 40 min

READY TO SERVE: 40 min

A Meal Worth Singing About

Spaghetti and meatballs is such an all-time favorite there's actually a song about it. You know the one, "On top of spaghetti, all covered with cheese, I lost my poor meatball, when somebody sneezed." Well, song or no song, you're going to have fun with this recipe because making homemade meatballs is like playing with clay but you get to eat your creations afterwards!

Whet your appetite with a picture of the finished meal so you know what the final product should look like.

Look here for fun background information about the featured recipe.

Check here to find out how much time you will need to prepare the recipe so you can plan mealtime accordingly.

Get Prepared! is the first section of the lesson. Review these four pages a day or more before you make the recipe.

Note to the Sous Chef
Provides a brief note to the sous chef about steps in the recipe that might require a little extra adult assistance or supervision.

Sneak Peek
This picture-guide provides a sneak peek of how the recipe goes together.

Note to the Chef
A brief note to let chefs know what there is to look forward to in the lesson.

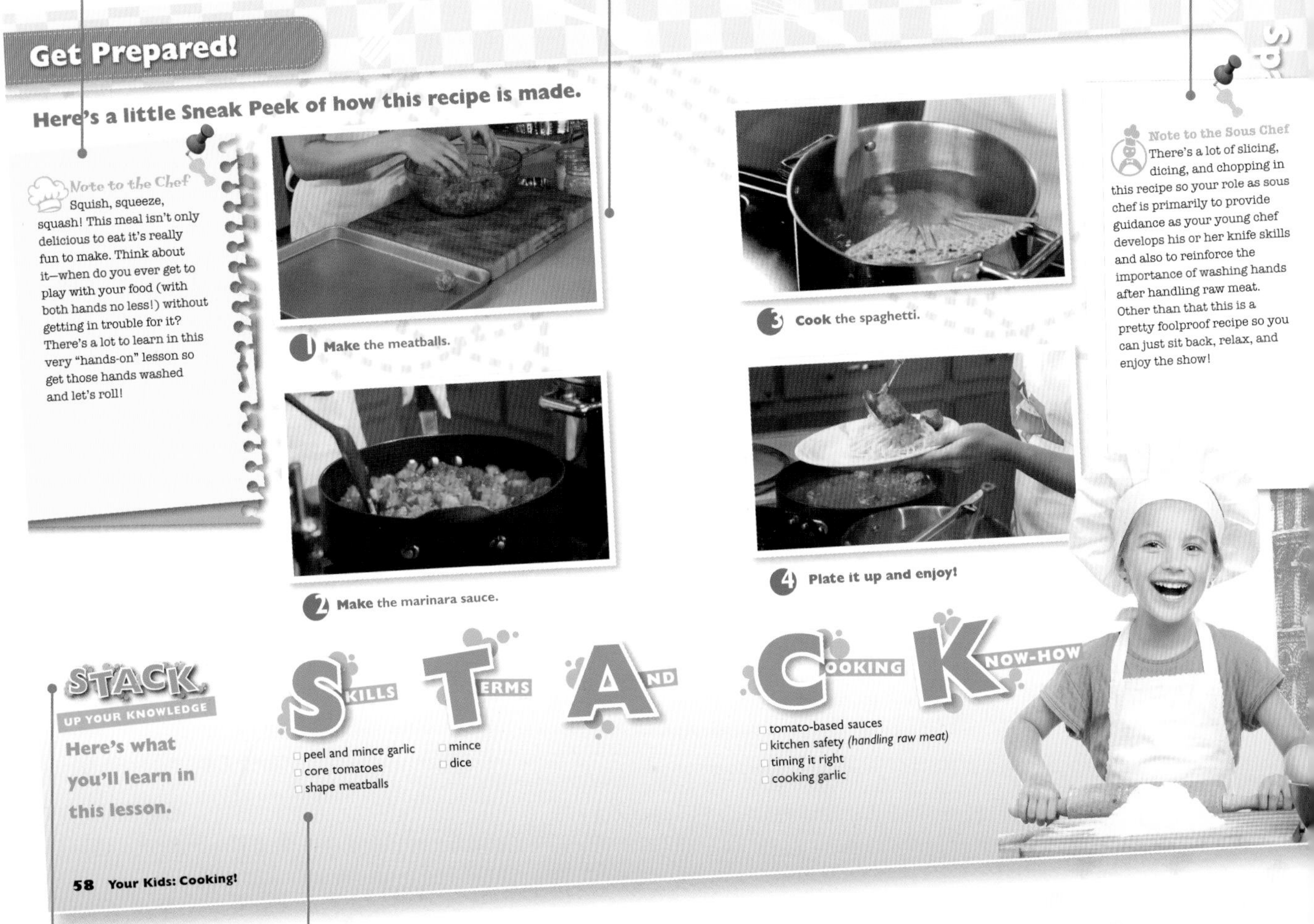
Get Prepared!

Here's a little Sneak Peek of how this recipe is made.

Note to the Chef
Squish, squeeze, squash! This meal isn't only delicious to eat it's really fun to make. Think about it—when do you ever get to play with your food (with both hands no less!) without getting in trouble for it? There's a lot to learn in this very "hands-on" lesson so get those hands washed and let's roll!

1 Make the meatballs.

2 Make the marinara sauce.

3 Cook the spaghetti.

4 Plate it up and enjoy!

Note to the Sous Chef
There's a lot of slicing, dicing, and chopping in this recipe so your role as sous chef is primarily to provide guidance as your young chef develops his or her knife skills and also to reinforce the importance of washing hands after handling raw meat. Other than that this is a pretty foolproof recipe so you can just sit back, relax, and enjoy the show!

STACK UP YOUR KNOWLEDGE
Here's what you'll learn in this lesson.

SKILLS
- peel and mince garlic
- core tomatoes
- shape meatballs

TERMS
- mince
- dice

AND

COOKING KNOW-HOW
- tomato-based sauces
- kitchen safety *(handling raw meat)*
- timing it right
- cooking garlic

58 Your Kids: Cooking!

Provides a preview of the STACK items taught in the lesson so chefs can focus their attention on the important new items they will be learning.

The STACK
"STACK" is an acronym for all the skills, terms, and cooking know-how taught in the lesson.

Shopping List

Check here to make sure you have everything you need before you start cooking. If no amount is indicated it means very little is needed. You can assume if you have the ingredient you will have enough to make the recipe.

What's On Your Plate?

This page provides basic nutrition information about the ingredients used to make the recipe, along with other healthy eating tips.

Get Prepared!

When you're ready to start cooking, watch Recipe 5: Spaghetti & Meatballs.

What You'll Need

. . . to make Spaghetti & Meatballs

Shopping List
- ground beef (1 lb)
- ground pork (½ lb)
- breadcrumbs
- Parmesan cheese (grated)
- egg (1)
- basil (dried)
- milk (½ cup)
- spaghetti noodles (1 lb)
- tomatoes (6 to 8 medium or 3 lb)
- onion (1 medium)
- garlic (2 or more cloves)
- sugar
- balsamic vinegar (optional)
- tomato paste (optional)

An Easy-Fix Option for this recipe can be downloaded for free at www.yourkidscooking.net

. . . and to

Complete Your Meal

garlic bread (oven-ready in a bag)
green salad (complete salad in a bag)

This meal provides protein, grains, and vegetables. But a fresh green salad goes great with spaghetti and it provides another excellent source of fresh, healthy vegetables.

Substitute two 15-oz cans of diced tomatoes to shorten the Get Set! time.

Shopping Tip

The type of tomato you use isn't as important as whether or not they are ripe. Choose tomatoes that are deep red in color, firm to the touch, and feel heavy for their size. Give them the smell test too—ripe tomatoes should smell like tomatoes!

60 Your Kids: Cooking!

Visit www.yourkidscooking.net to learn more!

What's On Your Plate?

Empty Calories: ground beef, ground pork
Fruits: none
Grains: pasta
Dairy: none
Protein: beef, pork
Vegetables: tomatoes, onions, lettuce

ChooseMyPlate.gov

Choose extra lean beef and pork to reduce the amount of empty calories from these foods.

In the Spotlight

Pasta is typically made with refined white flour, which is stripped of much of its nutrition during the refinement process. Whole-wheat pasta is a healthy and tasty alternative for this recipe.

Lettuce can be rich in vitamin K, which helps build strong bones. As a general rule, the darker green the leaves are, the more vitamins and minerals they contain. Iceberg lettuce has little nutritional value.

Olive oil is high in fat, but 85% is monounsaturated fat, which is essential to a healthy diet.

Why Whole Grains?

Eating whole grains, such as whole-wheat pasta, provides many health benefits and reduces the risk of some chronic diseases. Whole grains also contain a lot of fiber, making them a good fat-burning food. If you use whole-wheat pasta in dishes like spaghetti and meatballs, which are served with a rich and flavorful tomato-based sauce, you may not even taste the difference!

61

Spaghetti & Meatballs

Complete Your Meal

This handy feature offers suggestions for quick and easy side-dishes to serve with the main recipe to make it a nutritionally complete and balanced meal.

In the Spotlight

Check here for additional nutritional information about select ingredients.

ChooseMyPlate.gov

Learn how the ingredients used in the recipe contribute to a healthy and balanced plate. Ingredients suggested in the Complete Your Meal feature are shaded so you can see how they make the meal more nutritionally complete.

Easy-Fix Option

The Easy-Fix Option offers an optional preparation of the recipe using shortcuts that simplify the recipe preparation. The Easy-Fix Option recipes are available for free at **www.YourKidsCooking.net.**

Get Ready! is the first step of the recipe preparation. Complete this step after watching the *Get Ready!* segment on the DVD.

Get Set! is the second step of the recipe preparation when all the prep work is done. Complete these steps after watching the *Get Set!* segment on the DVD.

DVD Prompt
Lets you know which segment of the DVD to watch before completing the steps in the book.

Ingredients
List and pictures of ingredients needed to make the recipe.

Utensils
List and pictures of utensils needed to make the recipe.

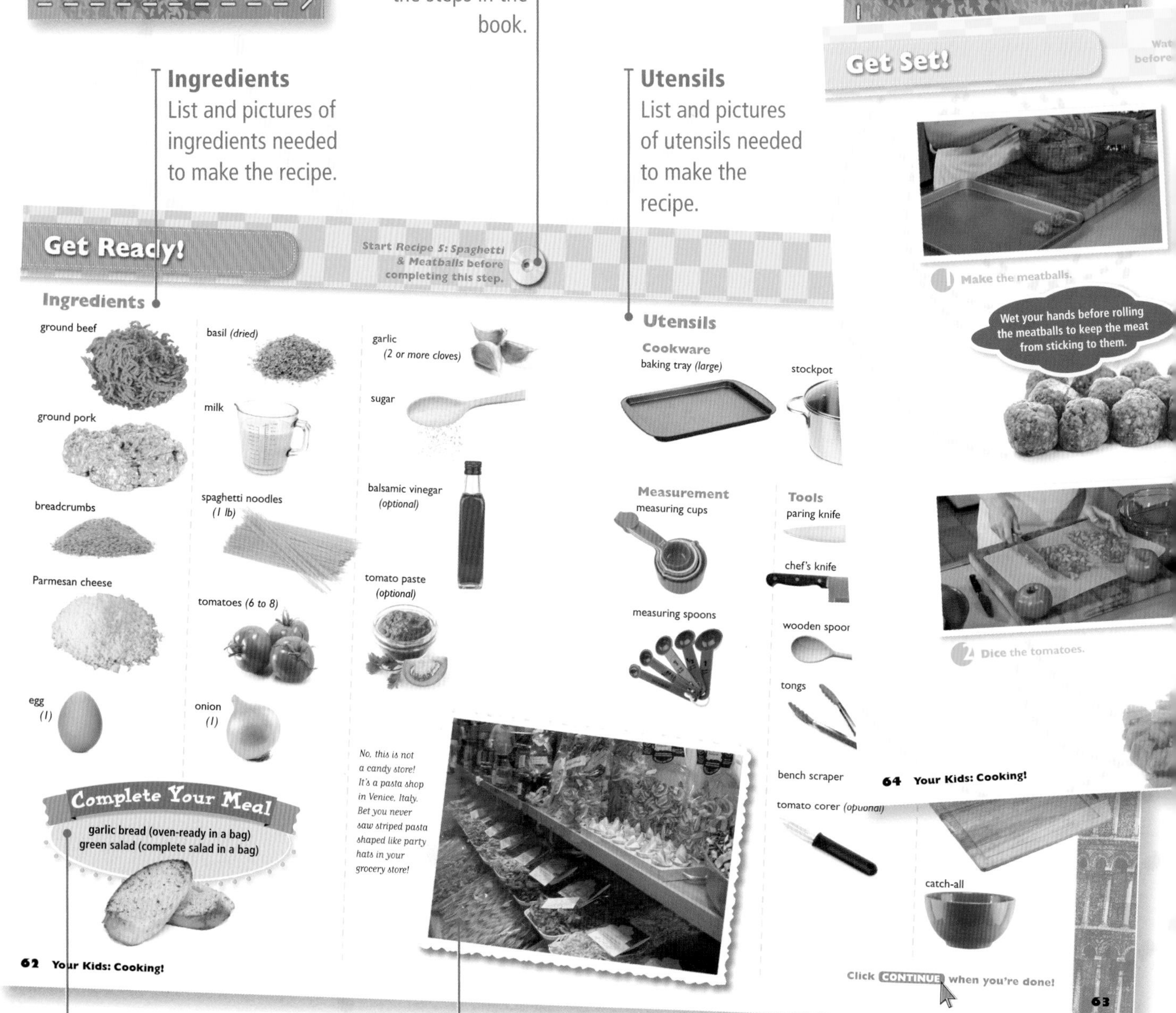

Get Ready!
Start Recipe 5: Spaghetti & Meatballs before completing this step.
Ingredients
ground beef
ground pork
breadcrumbs
Parmesan cheese
egg (1)
basil (dried)
milk
spaghetti noodles (1 lb)
tomatoes (6 to 8)
onion (1)
garlic (2 or more cloves)
sugar
balsamic vinegar (optional)
tomato paste (optional)
Complete Your Meal
garlic bread (oven-ready in a bag)
green salad (complete salad in a bag)
No, this is not a candy store! It's a pasta shop in Venice, Italy. Bet you never saw striped pasta shaped like party hats in your grocery store!
62 Your Kids: Cooking!
Utensils
Cookware
baking tray (large)
stockpot
Measurement
measuring cups
measuring spoons
Tools
paring knife
chef's knife
wooden spoon
tongs
bench scraper
tomato corer (optional)
catch-all
Click CONTINUE when you're done!
63
Get Set!
Make the meatballs.
Wet your hands before rolling the meatballs to keep the meat from sticking to them.
Dice the tomatoes.
64 Your Kids: Cooking!

Complete Your Meal
A reminder of the additional ingredients you will need if you have chosen to make the suggested side-dishes.

Cooking Around the World
Look here for fun and interesting cooking-related tidbits from around the globe.

Kid-Friendly Recipe Format
Unique recipe format with pictures of every step makes it easy for kids to complete the steps all on their own.

Get Cooking! is the third step of the recipe preparation when the cooking starts. Complete these steps after watching the *Get Cooking!* segment on the DVD.

Make sure you take pictures as you go through the steps!

Spaghetti & Meatballs

3 Chop the onion.
- chop onion into ¼-inch pieces

4 Peel and mince the garlic.
- cut root end off 2–5 garlic cloves
- smash cloves under a flat surface to remove peel
- mince into tiny pieces

Complete Your Meal Reminder
A reminder for when the sous chef should prepare the optional side-dishes.

Get Cooking!

Watch the *Get Cooking!* segment before completing these steps.

Make sure you take pictures as you go through the steps!

Spaghetti & Meatballs

1 Bake the meatballs.
- bake meatballs uncovered at 325°F
- set a timer for 15 minutes

2 Make the marinara sauce.
- cook onions in **1 Tbsp** olive oil
- add tomatoes and:
  - **2 tsp salt**
  - **2–3 tsp basil**
  - **1 tsp sugar**
- simmer uncovered 15–20 minutes, stirring occasionally

3 Cook the pasta.
- cook spaghetti according to directions on package

4 Finish the marinara sauce.
- when meatballs are completely cooked, add to marinara sauce
- turn off burner; cover pan to keep meatballs warm

5 Drain the pasta.
- drain spaghetti; return to stockpot
- drizzle a little olive oil onto pasta to keep it from sticking together

Complete Your Meal
Ask your sous chef to prepare the green salad while the pasta cooks. Heat the garlic bread after the meatballs are done.

6 Plate it up and enjoy!
- top a serving of spaghetti with meatballs and sauce
- garnish with grated Parmesan cheese
- serve with garlic bread and fresh green salad

Happy Eating!

66 Your Kids: Cooking!

67

Visit **www.yourkidscooking.net** to learn more!

Test Your Skills! provides an opportunity for young chefs to practice their new skills making a recipe very similar to the target recipe.

STACK Reminder
Using the STACK chart to track progress reinforces the chef's sense of accomplishment and builds motivation.

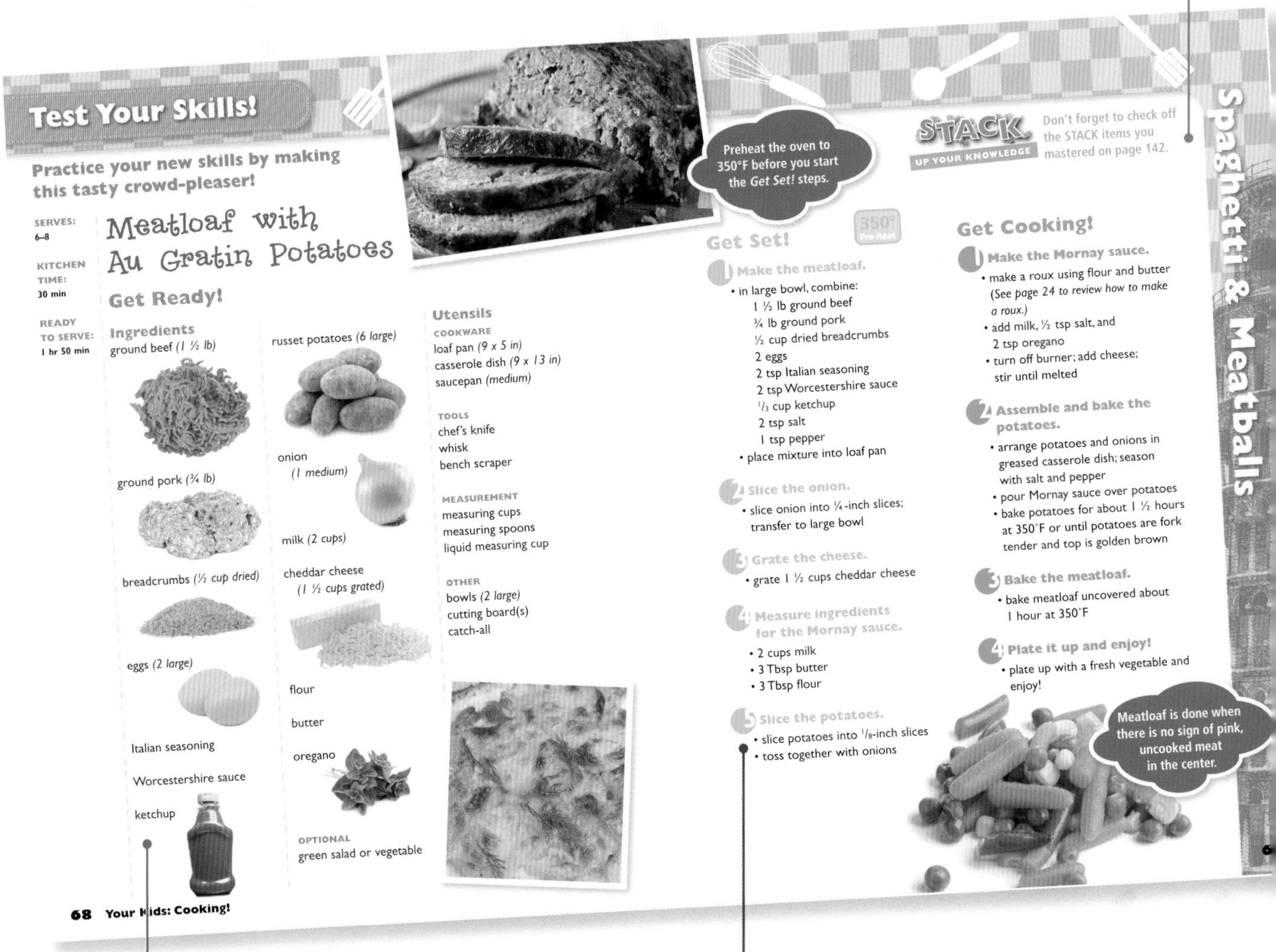

Test Your Skills!

Practice your new skills by making this tasty crowd-pleaser!

SERVES: 6–8

KITCHEN TIME: 30 min

READY TO SERVE: 1 hr 50 min

Meatloaf with Au Gratin Potatoes

Get Ready!

Ingredients

ground beef *(1 ½ lb)*

ground pork *(¾ lb)*

breadcrumbs *(½ cup dried)*

eggs *(2 large)*

Italian seasoning

Worcestershire sauce

ketchup

russet potatoes *(6 large)*

onion *(1 medium)*

milk *(2 cups)*

cheddar cheese *(1 ½ cups grated)*

flour

butter

oregano

OPTIONAL

green salad or vegetable

Utensils

COOKWARE

loaf pan *(9 x 5 in)*

casserole dish *(9 x 13 in)*

saucepan *(medium)*

TOOLS

chef's knife

whisk

bench scraper

MEASUREMENT

measuring cups

measuring spoons

liquid measuring cup

OTHER

bowls *(2 large)*

cutting board(s)

catch-all

Preheat the oven to 350°F before you start the *Get Set!* steps.

STACK UP YOUR KNOWLEDGE — Don't forget to check off the STACK items you mastered on page 142.

Get Set!

350° Pre-heat

1. **Make the meatloaf.**
   - in large bowl, combine:
     1 ½ lb ground beef
     ¾ lb ground pork
     ½ cup dried breadcrumbs
     2 eggs
     2 tsp Italian seasoning
     2 tsp Worcestershire sauce
     ⅓ cup ketchup
     2 tsp salt
     1 tsp pepper
   - place mixture into loaf pan
2. **Slice the onion.**
   - slice onion into ¼-inch slices; transfer to large bowl
3. **Grate the cheese.**
   - grate 1 ½ cups cheddar cheese
4. **Measure ingredients for the Mornay sauce.**
   - 2 cups milk
   - 3 Tbsp butter
   - 3 Tbsp flour
5. **Slice the potatoes.**
   - slice potatoes into ⅛-inch slices
   - toss together with onions

Get Cooking!

1. **Make the Mornay sauce.**
   - make a roux using flour and butter *(See page 24 to review how to make a roux.)*
   - add milk, ½ tsp salt, and 2 tsp oregano
   - turn off burner; add cheese; stir until melted
2. **Assemble and bake the potatoes.**
   - arrange potatoes and onions in greased casserole dish; season with salt and pepper
   - pour Mornay sauce over potatoes
   - bake potatoes for about 1 ½ hours at 350°F or until potatoes are fork tender and top is golden brown
3. **Bake the meatloaf.**
   - bake meatloaf uncovered about 1 hour at 350°F
4. **Plate it up and enjoy!**
   - plate up with a fresh vegetable and enjoy!

Meatloaf is done when there is no sign of pink, uncooked meat in the center.

Spaghetti & Meatballs

68 Your Kids: Cooking!

***Get Ready!* Ingredient List**
Ingredient amounts are indicated on the *Get Ready!* list so you can use it as a shopping list.

***Get Set! / Get Cooking!* Steps**
Directions are written in the same step-by-step, kid-friendly format so chefs can complete the recipe with ease, even without a video demonstration.

Reward Yourself! offers a sweet treat or snack recipe for chefs to make to reward themselves for a job well done.

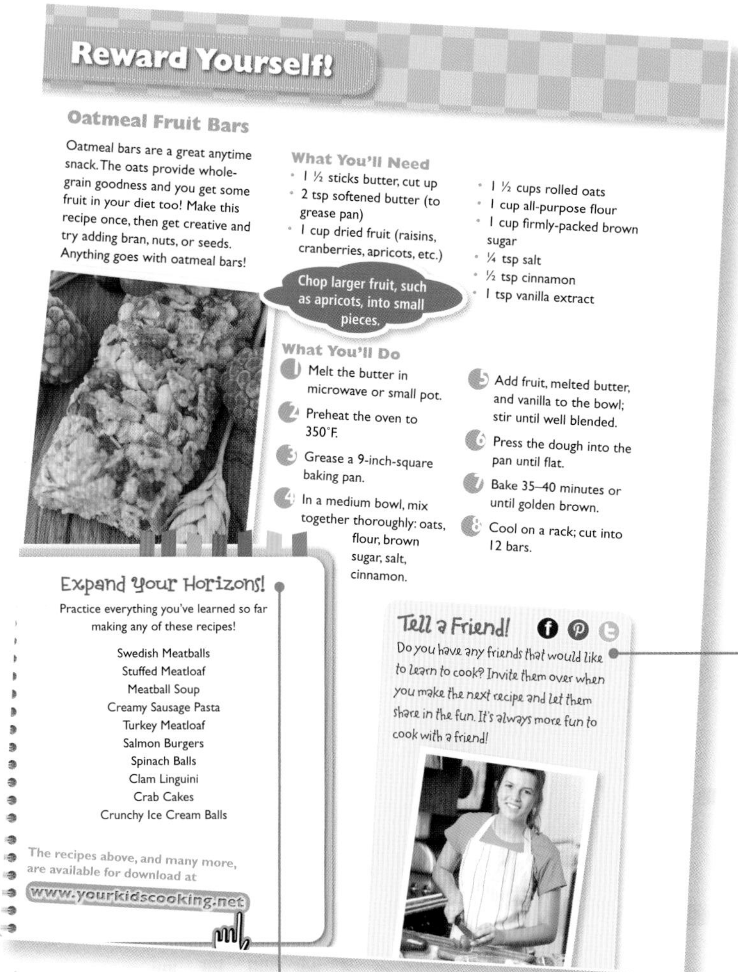

Reward Yourself!

Oatmeal Fruit Bars

Oatmeal bars are a great anytime snack. The oats provide whole-grain goodness and you get some fruit in your diet too! Make this recipe once, then get creative and try adding bran, nuts, or seeds. Anything goes with oatmeal bars!

What You'll Need

- 1 ½ sticks butter, cut up
- 2 tsp softened butter (to grease pan)
- 1 cup dried fruit (raisins, cranberries, apricots, etc.)
- 1 ½ cups rolled oats
- 1 cup all-purpose flour
- 1 cup firmly-packed brown sugar
- ¼ tsp salt
- ½ tsp cinnamon
- 1 tsp vanilla extract

Chop larger fruit, such as apricots, into small pieces.

What You'll Do

1. Melt the butter in microwave or small pot.
2. Preheat the oven to 350°F.
3. Grease a 9-inch-square baking pan.
4. In a medium bowl, mix together thoroughly: oats, flour, brown sugar, salt, cinnamon.
5. Add fruit, melted butter, and vanilla to the bowl; stir until well blended.
6. Press the dough into the pan until flat.
7. Bake 35–40 minutes or until golden brown.
8. Cool on a rack; cut into 12 bars.

Expand Your Horizons!

Practice everything you've learned so far making any of these recipes!

Swedish Meatballs
Stuffed Meatloaf
Meatball Soup
Creamy Sausage Pasta
Turkey Meatloaf
Salmon Burgers
Spinach Balls
Clam Linguini
Crab Cakes
Crunchy Ice Cream Balls

The recipes above, and many more, are available for download at www.yourkidscooking.net

Tell a Friend!

Do you have any friends that would like to learn to cook? Invite them over when you make the next recipe and let them share in the fun. It's always more fun to cook with a friend!

Tell a Friend!
Suggestions for ways chefs can share their success and enthusiasm with friends and family and inspire others to join in the fun of learning to cook.

Expand Your Horizons
This is a list of ten recipes kids can make to continue practicing and developing their cooking skills. These recipes are available on our website and written in the same easy-to-follow format as the *Test Your Skills!* recipe.

Get Your Kitchen Ready!

Here are all the utensils you will need to complete the 20 recipes in the book. A complete Kitchen Equipment Buyer's Guide with tips and suggestions for how to choose the right tools for your kitchen can be found on our website at **www.YourKidsCooking.net.**

	French Toast	Macaroni & Cheese	Tamale Pie	Quiche	Spaghetti & Meatballs

COOKWARE	griddle 	stock pot sauce pan (large) baking dish (9 x 13 in)	sauté pan (large, nonstick) casserole dish (10 x 10 in)	frying pan pie plate (9-in glass or ceramic)	baking tray (large) 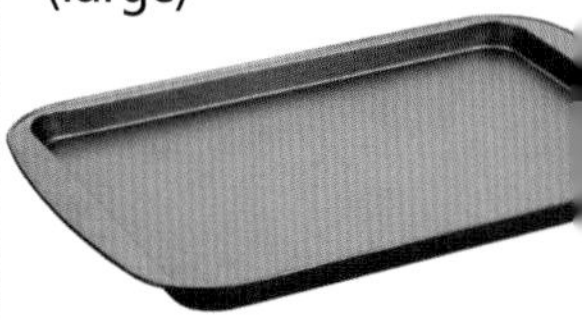
TOOLS	whisk rubber spatula sieve (optional) 	cheese grater rubber spatula straightedge (optional)	chef's knife can opener bench scraper (optional)	rolling pin pastry blender 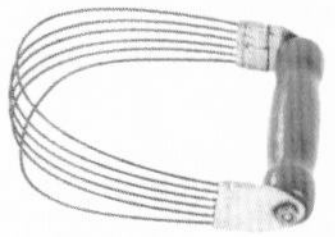	paring knife tongs wooden spoon 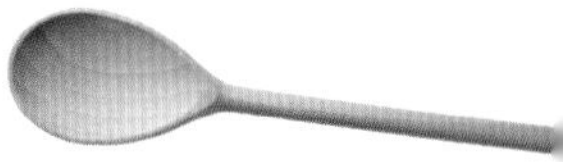
MEASUREMENT	measuring spoons liquid measuring cup, small (1–2 cups)	—	liquid measuring cup (3–4 cup, large) dry measuring cups 	—	—
OTHER	flat-bottomed bowl catch-all[1] 	colander bowls (2 small) cutting board 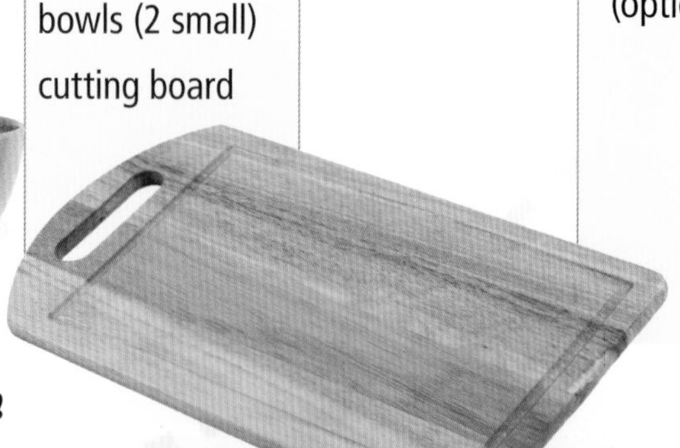	—	pastry cloth (optional)	—

[1] A small bowl to hold cooking scraps and trash.

[2] A large frying pan can be used instead of a wok.

[3] You can make a double-boiler by placing a metal or glass bowl in a large saucepan. The bottom of the bowl should be about 2"above the bottom of the pan.

[4] A pan with a non-stick surface will not work for making a pan sauce.

[5] A large stock pot with a tight-fitting lid can be used if you don't have a Dutch oven.

	Stir-Fry 	Eggs Benedict 	Chicken Parmesan 	Pork Chops 	Pot Roast 
COOKWARE	wok[2] 	double-boiler[3]	—	sauté pan[4] (large, stainless steel)	Dutch oven[5] 
TOOLS	vegetable peeler 	slotted spoon 	cheese slicer (wire) meat tenderizer	—	potato masher 
MEASUREMENT	–				
OTHER	–				

Here are suggestions for a few additional items that will help make meal preparation easier:

- Ramekins for holding kosher salt and ground pepper.
- Several other ramekins and custard cups for holding smaller quantities of measured ingredients.

- Oil dispensers for your most frequently used oils.
- A utensil crock for storing frequently used utensils.

- A knife block with kitchen scissors.
- Several cotton dish clothes that you can dampen and use to clean your work area as you go.
- One or two spoon rests.

Kitchen Safety

Be sure to also watch the Knife Safety Segment on the DVD for a demonstration of the safety tips below.

It is said that the kitchen is the most dangerous room in your house. But if you're aware of the potential dangers and how to avoid them, it can also be one of the most fun rooms in your house! The dangers in the kitchen come from sharp stuff, hot stuff, and germy stuff. Read over the safety tips below with your sous chef, ask questions about anything you don't understand, and then be confident that you're ready to have a safe and enjoyable cooking experience.

Sharp Stuff

- Always have adult supervision or permission when using a knife.
- Always carry a knife with the blade pointing down.
- When using a cheese grater, be careful to keep your fingers away from the metal bumps.
- Canned food lids are very sharp! Use a fork or other utensil to lift lids from the can.
- When using a vegetable peeler, be careful to keep your fingers out of the way of the blades.
- Point the knife blade away from your body when you cut, not towards it.
- Never cut anything while holding it in your hand. Place food on a cutting board to cut.

As the supervising adult, it is the sous chef's responsibility to determine if the chef is ready to use a knife. Read these knife safety tips together and make sure the chef understands the importance of each one.

Hot Stuff

- Always turn pan handles toward the middle of the stove so you won't accidentally bump the handle and knock over the pan.
- Turn your face away from the sink when draining hot water from a pot. The hot steam can burn you!
- Never leave utensils in the pot or pan while food is cooking.
- Remember that hot food of any kind can burn you, including water, soups, sauces, butter and oil.

Germy Stuff

- Wash your hands in warm, soapy water *before* you start cooking or handling any type of food.
- Wash your hands in warm, soapy water *after* handling raw meat, fish, or poultry.
- Wash all utensils, including cutting boards, after using them on raw meat, fish, or poultry.
- Do not let raw meat, fish, poultry, or eggs touch other ingredients.
- Do not put cooked meat, fish, or poultry back on the same plate or tray it was on before you cooked it.
- Wash all vegetables and fruit before using them.

Safe-Kitchen Rules

There are just two rules we ask that you follow when enjoying the YKC cooking program.

Rule #1: Always have the supervision of your sous chef (parent or other adult) when completing the lessons.

Rule #2: Always follow rule #1!

Note to the Sous Chef

Kids enjoy cooking more when they are allowed to be in charge of the process. And with you acting as their sous chef, they will receive all the support and encouragement they need to proceed with confidence. We want your experience with our program to be a great one, so we offer a few suggestions that will help to make this shared learning adventure as enjoyable and successful as possible.

Be Prepared

Although YKC is easy to use, it is quite unique in its approach to teaching kids to cook. Knowing what to expect and understanding how the recipe-lessons work are the key to success. Before getting started with the recipe-lessons, make sure you have answered any questions the young chef may have about the information in the *Let's Get Acquainted!* section.

View Mistakes as Opportunities to Learn

Things are bound to go wrong once in a while. Things may get burned or broken, and messes will be made. But that's okay! Mistakes happen. The trick is to view them as opportunities to learn and improve. Learning how to deal with failure teaches kids strategies to figure out what went wrong and how to do better next time.

Be Supportive Without Taking Over

Kids can and will rise to meet any appropriate challenge—if we let them! There is a fine line between providing help and taking over. Unless it's a matter of your child's safety, try to offer help only when asked for it. Kids learn by doing, and the more they do, the more they learn. The amount of pride kids feel in their accomplishments is directly related to the degree to which they are responsible for them.

Clean As You Go

To keep after-meal clean up to a minimum, prepare some warm, soapy dishwater right from the start. There's always some down time waiting for things to heat up or cool down. Use this time to wash a few dishes and after-meal clean up is a breeze. And remember, many hands make light work!

Provide Opportunities to Apply New Skills

Practice makes perfect, so provide additional opportunities for your young chef to put their new skills to work making the recipes provided in the *Expand Your Horizons!* section on our website. With ten recipes to choose from after completing each recipe-lesson, there are lots of delicious ways to keep the learning alive.

Reflect on the Learning Experience

Talking about an experience afterwards is not only fun, it's also a great way to learn more from it. Discuss what went right and laugh about what went wrong. Think about what you might do differently next time. Record your reflections in the journal pages in the back of the book and use them to guide you to even greater success in the future.

Have Fun!

Cooking should be fun, not a chore. And learning to cook is an adventure that can last a lifetime. Embrace the adventure with a spirit of discovery and the joy of excitement about venturing into uncharted territory. It's all about the journey, not the destination, so have fun and enjoy every twist and turn along the way.

Let the Cooking Begin!

LESSON 1

French Toast

SERVES: 2–4

COMPLETE THE LESSON: 25 min

READY TO SERVE: 25 min

A Royal Breakfast

You're going to just love making. . . and eating. . . French toast. It's quick. It's easy. But mostly, it's deeeeelicious! A breakfast fit for a king, or a queen. . . or both! In fact, French toast was served to European royalty as far back as 1670. That's almost 400 years ago! Anything that's been around that long must be yummy, right?

Get Prepared!

Here's a little Sneak Peek of how this recipe is made.

Note to the Chef

Hey chefs, here we go! Are you ready for some fun? The main goal of this recipe-lesson is to familiarize you with basic measuring tools and techniques. You'll also learn about making sure you're cooking food at the right temperature. This is one of the most important things a chef needs to know. Once you've mastered these basics, you'll be ready to make all kinds of grilled sandwiches, scrambled eggs, fried egg sandwiches, and so much more. So, roll up your sleeves, grab your sous chef, and let the fun begin!

1 **Whisk** eggs, milk, and flavorings together.

2 **Soak** slices of bread in the egg mixture.

STACK UP YOUR KNOWLEDGE

Here's what you'll learn in this lesson.

SKILLS

- ☐ crack eggs
- ☐ whisk eggs
- ☐ use measuring spoons
- ☐ measure liquids
- ☐ flip food with a spatula

TERMS

- ☐ whisk
- ☐ dust
- ☐ flat spatula

3 **Pan-fry** the bread.

4 **Plate it up** and enjoy!

Note to the Sous Chef
This recipe is relatively simple to make, so little help is needed from the sous chef. The most difficult skill for kids to master is flipping the French toast. If your young chef has trouble with this, have her or him practice with a plain piece of bread. Also, because all stoves are different, finding the right heat setting on your particular stove takes experience your young chef has not yet developed, so your help may be needed with this as well.

COOKING KNOW-HOW

- ☐ preheating pans
- ☐ cooking with butter
- ☐ pan-frying

Get Prepared!

Wait to watch *Recipe 1: French Toast* until you are ready to start cooking.

What You'll Need . . .

to make French Toast

Hawaiian sweet bread, raisin bread or any bread enriched with eggs and butter, such as brioche or Challah, works best.

Shopping List

- bread (4 slices)
- eggs (3)
- sugar
- cinnamon
- vanilla
- butter
- syrup
- powdered sugar

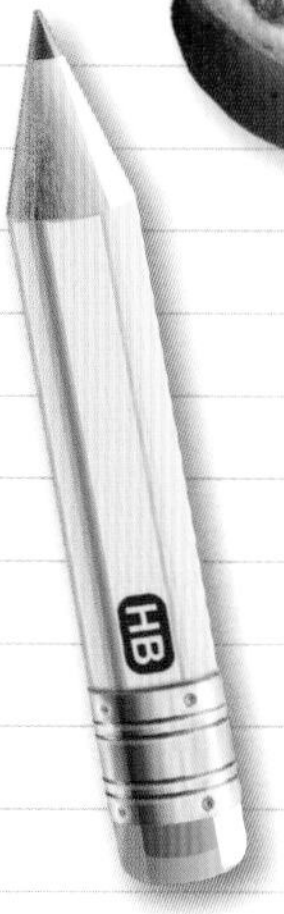

An Easy-Fix Option for this recipe can be downloaded for free at

www.yourkidscooking.net

. . . and to Complete Your Meal

fresh fruit | fruit juice
pre-cooked sausage links

A healthy breakfast includes fresh fruit or 100% fruit juice and 8 ounces of a dairy product, such as skim milk or yogurt. For a little extra boost of protein, serve with a couple of lean, pre-cooked sausage links.

Always wash fresh fruit before serving.

Shopping Tip

When buying eggs, always open the carton to make sure none of the eggs are cracked. Also, check the "sell-by" date on the carton. Eggs will last up to three weeks after the sell-by date. Storing them in their original carton makes it easy to judge their freshness.

Visit www.yourkidscooking.net to learn more!

What's On Your Plate?

Include milk as a beverage at meals. Choose fat-free or low-fat milk to lower saturated fat and calories without reducing calcium and essential nutrients.

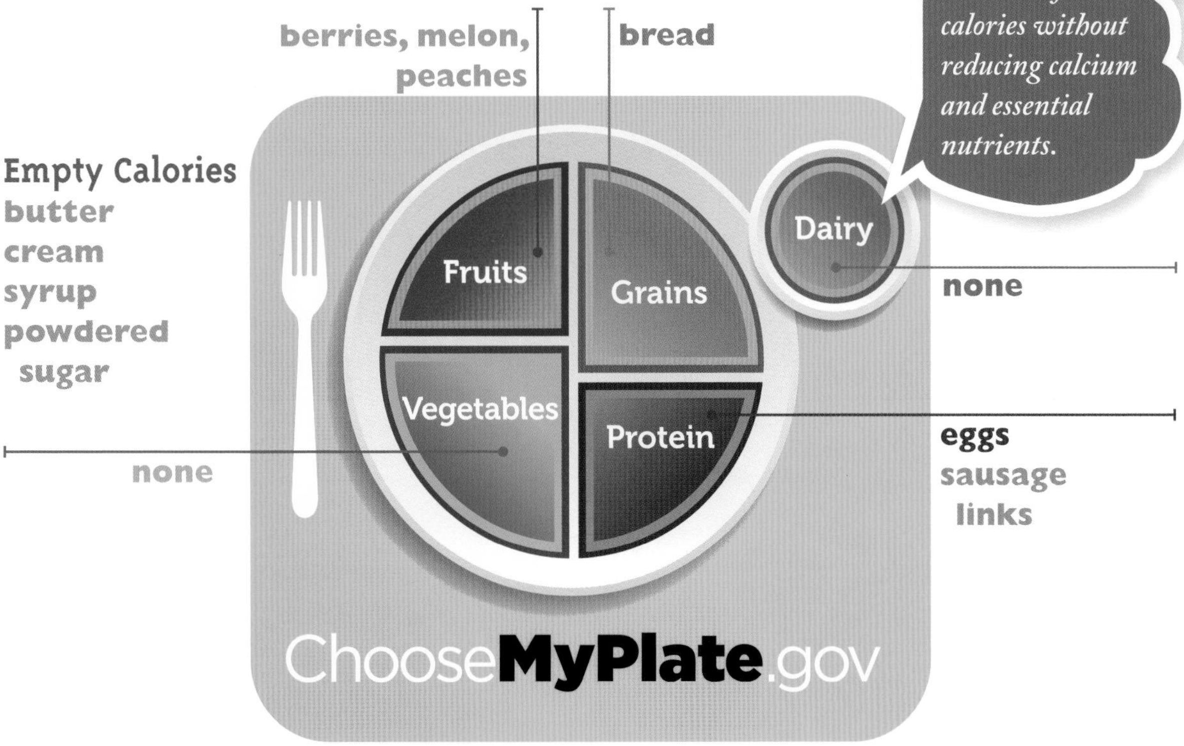

Understanding Empty Calories

The term "empty calories" refers to calories that are "empty" of nutritional value. They are found in solid fats, such as butter and cream, and in sugary foods such as syrup and powdered sugar. A small amount of empty calories is okay, but you should limit how many you eat. Eating too many empty calories makes it hard to avoid eating more calories than you need.

In the Spotlight

Sausage links are typically made from pork and tend to be high in fat and cholesterol. Leaner varieties made from turkey or chicken provide a healthy alternative.

Breads such as Challah or Hawaiian sweet bread are made with refined white flour, not whole-grain flour. Refined grains have had the bran and germ removed, which also removes dietary fiber, iron, and many B vitamins. Check the ingredient list for the words "whole grain" or "whole wheat" to decide if foods are made from a whole grain.

Get Ready!

Start *Recipe 1: French Toast* before completing this step.

Ingredients

bread *(4 slices)*

eggs *(3)*

milk *(or cream)*

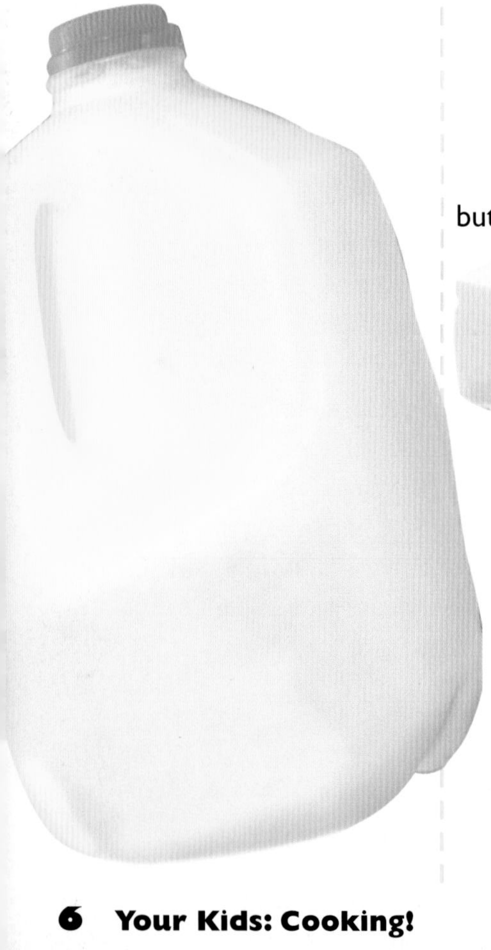

sugar

cinnamon

vanilla

butter

syrup

powdered sugar

Complete Your Meal

fresh fruit | 100% fruit juice

pre-cooked sausage links

Utensils

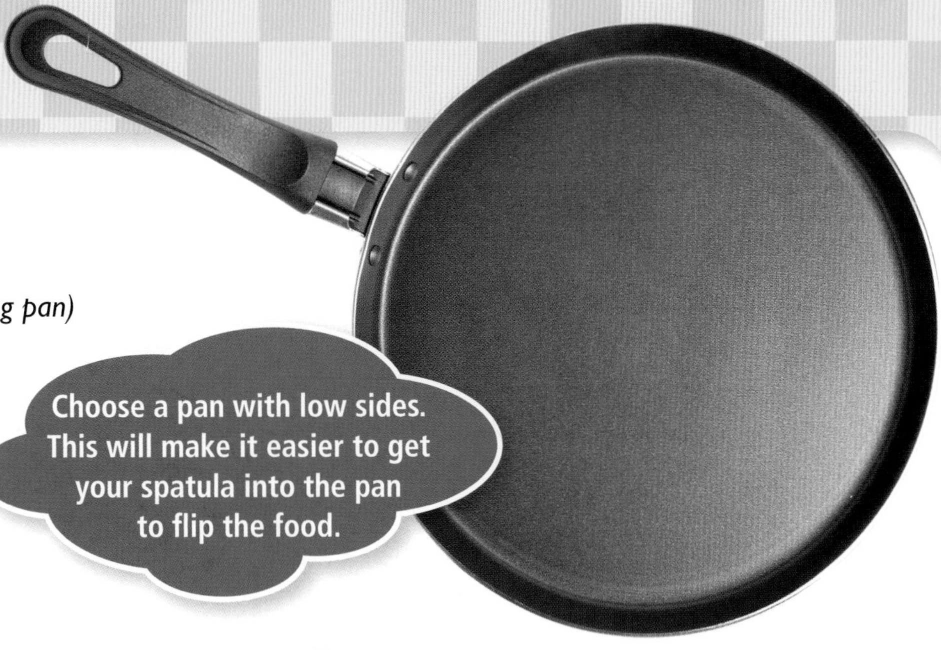

Cookware
griddle *(or large frying pan)*

Choose a pan with low sides. This will make it easier to get your spatula into the pan to flip the food.

Measurement
measuring spoons

liquid measuring cup

Tools
whisk

flat spatula

sieve *(or small spoon)*

Other
flat-bottomed bowl

catch-all *(small)*

Griddles are used all around the world and come in all shapes and sizes. The griddle in this picture is being used by an Ethiopian woman to cook injera, a traditional African flatbread.

Click CONTINUE when you're done!

Get Set!

Watch the *Get Set!* segment before completing these steps.

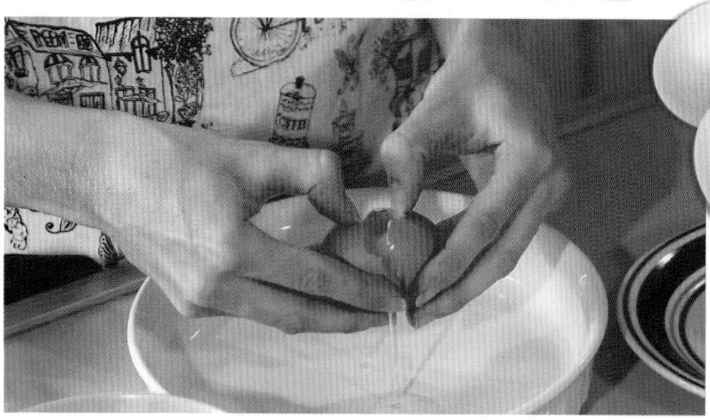

- crack **3 eggs** into the flat-bottomed bowl

1 Crack the eggs.

- measure ¼ **cup milk** into a liquid measuring cup
- add the milk to the eggs

2 Measure the milk.

- whisk the eggs and milk until they are thoroughly combined

3 Whisk the eggs and milk.

"Thoroughly combined" means there is no sign of gooey egg white or yellow egg yolk.

- add **1 Tbsp sugar** to the egg mixture

4 Measure the sugar.

Possible abbreviations for tablespoon are *Tbsp*, *Tbls*, or *T*. The abbreviation for teaspoon is either *tsp* or *t*.

- add **1 tsp cinnamon** to the egg mixture

5 Measure the cinnamon.

Measure over your catch-all to avoid spilling into the egg mixture.

- add ¼ **tsp vanilla** to the egg mixture
- whisk once more to combine ingredients

6 Measure the vanilla.

Click CONTINUE when you're done!

Get Cooking!

Watch the *Get Cooking!* segment before completing these steps.

Butter burns easily! When cooking with butter, cook food slowly over medium heat to avoid burning.

- set the burner to medium heat
- let the pan heat up for about a minute

1 Preheat the griddle.

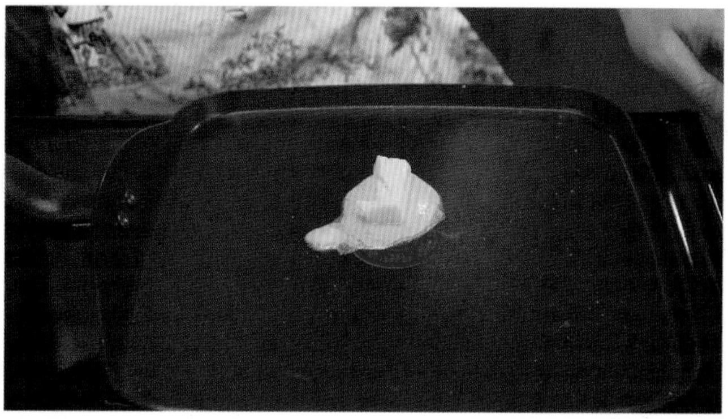

If the butter is melting too quickly, remove pan from burner to cool and adjust the heat as necessary.

- add **1 Tbsp butter** to the hot pan

2 Melt the butter.

- soak both sides of the bread in the egg mixture

3 Soak the bread slices.

Complete Your Meal

Ask your sous chef to prepare the fruit while you're cooking the French toast.

- cook the bread for 3–4 minutes, until it turns golden-brown

4 Cook the bread.

The key to successful pan-frying is cooking food at the right temperature. Adjust heat as necessary to maintain proper cooking temperature.

- flip the French toast and cook another 3–4 minutes

5 Flip the bread.

- drizzle with syrup
- dust with powdered sugar

6 Plate it up and enjoy!

Happy Eating!

Test Your Skills!

Here's another fun and delicious recipe you can make to practice your new skills.

SERVES:
1

KITCHEN TIME:
10 min

READY TO SERVE:
10 min

Fried Egg Sandwich

Get Ready!

Ingredients

egg *(1 per sandwich)*

bread *(2 slices per sandwich)*

American cheese slice *(1 per sandwich)*

ham slice *(1 per sandwich)*

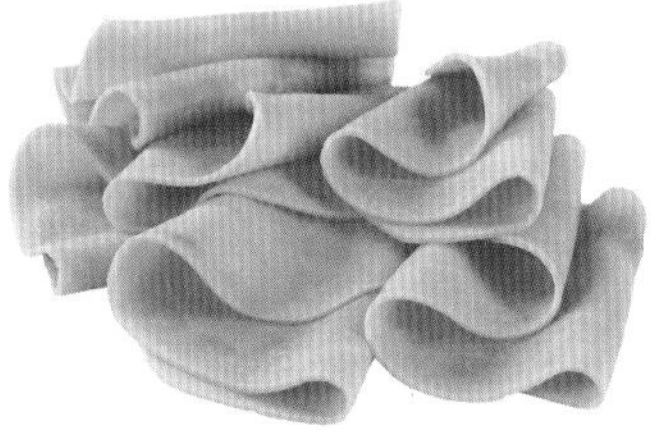

butter *(softened to room temperature)*

OPTIONAL

frozen hash browns

fruit juice

Utensils

COOKWARE

frying pan

TOOLS

flat spatula

butter knife

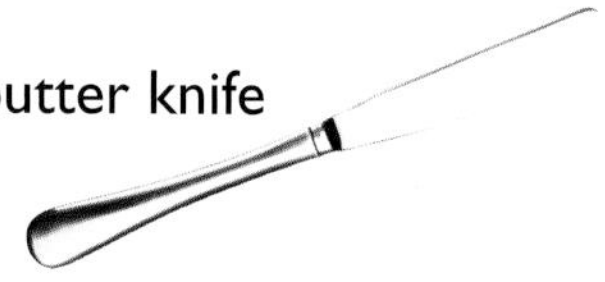

OTHER

glass or jar with opening slightly smaller than the slice of bread

catch-all

STACK UP YOUR KNOWLEDGE

Don't forget to check off the STACK items you mastered on page 142.

Get Set!

1 Preheat frying pan.

- set burner to medium heat

2 Prepare bread slices.

- cut out a circle from the center of one slice of bread using the rim of the glass or jar
- spread butter on one side of both slices of bread

Try using a heart-shaped cookie cutter to cut out the opening in the bread.

Complete Your Meal

Have your sous chef prepare the hash browns while you make the sandwiches.

Get Cooking!

1 Melt the butter.

- melt 1 Tbsp butter over medium heat

2 Fry the egg.

- place bread slice with hole cut out, unbuttered-side down in the pan
- crack 1 egg into the hole in the bread; season with salt and pepper to taste
- cook until egg white has set, then flip

3 Finish cooking the sandwich.

- place a slice of ham and cheese over the egg
- top with the other slice of bread, butter-side out
- cook until golden brown, then flip the sandwich
- cook 2–3 minutes until cheese melts and bread turns golden brown

4 Plate it up and enjoy!

- plate up and enjoy with some hash browns and fruit juice

Reward Yourself!

Fruit Smoothie

Smoothies are a great way to start the morning or to get recharged during the day. They are made with all sorts of healthy goodies and are low in fat so indulge yourself with one of these frothy fruit delights everyday. But watch out . . . they can be habit forming!

What You'll Need

- 1 cup vanilla yogurt
- ¼ cup orange or other fruit juice
- 1 cup fresh or frozen fruit of your choice

What You'll Do

1. Combine all ingredients in a blender.
2. Blend until smooth; add more juice as necessary to adjust thickness.

Use low- or fat-free yogurt to reduce the amount of empty calories.

Bananas that are overripe can be frozen and then used later in smoothies. Allow frozen bananas to thaw for 30 minutes for easy peeling.

If you are using fresh fruit, add 4 or 5 ice cubes.

Expand Your Horizons!

Practice everything you've learned so far by making one or all of these delicious recipes.

Grilled Cheese Sandwich
Pigs In A Blanket
Breakfast Blintzes
Fried Eggs
Scrambled Eggs
Cheese Omelet
Grilled PBJ
Grilled Cuban Sandwich
Monte Cristo Sandwich
Baked French Toast

The recipes above, and many more, are available for download at

www.yourkidscooking.net

Tell a Friend!

Be an inspiration to others! Ask your sous chef to share pictures of your culinary success with friends and family on their favorite social networking sites.

LESSON 2

Macaroni & Cheese

SERVES: 8–10

COMPLETE THE LESSON: 30 min

READY TO SERVE: 45 min

Macaroni & Cheese— A Crayon Color?

That's right! Macaroni & cheese is such a favorite among kids that there's actually a crayon color named after it! But you're not going to be making the kind out of the box. In this lesson you'll learn how to make homemade macaroni & cheese, which is not only healthier for you, it's also way tastier!

Get Prepared!

Here's a little Sneak Peek of how this recipe is made.

Note to the Chef

Even though homemade macaroni and cheese is really easy to make, there's a lot to be learned. This lesson teaches you how to cook pasta, make a cheese sauce, and measure accurately—skills no chef can afford to be without! Once you've mastered these basics, making recipes like fettuccini Alfredo, pasta salad, and nacho cheese sauce will be a snap!

1 **Cook** the pasta.

2 **Make** a cheese sauce from milk, butter, flour, and cheese.

STACK UP YOUR KNOWLEDGE

Here's what you'll learn in this lesson.

SKILLS

- ☐ grate cheese
- ☐ measure liquids
- ☐ measure dry ingredients

TERMS

- ☐ roux
- ☐ rubber spatula
- ☐ colander
- ☐ simmer
- ☐ full boil
- ☐ slow boil

A N

3 **Combine** cheese sauce and pasta.

4 **Apply** the topping and bake for 15 minutes.

Note to the Sous Chef
Though homemade macaroni and cheese is really very simple to make, there are a couple of steps the new chef may need some help with. Pay particular attention when it's time to drain the pasta. The water is hot and the pan is heavy so make sure to provide assistance as needed. Also, when it's time to pour the pasta into the baking dish, the pan might be too heavy for younger chefs to manage safely. Be ready to assist if necessary.

Cooking Know-How

- ☐ cooking pasta
- ☐ kitchen safety *(draining pasta)*
- ☐ how to make a cheese sauce
- ☐ thickening sauces
- ☐ baking casseroles

Get Prepared!

When you're ready to start cooking, watch *Recipe 2: Macaroni & Cheese.*

What You'll Need

. . . to make Mac & Cheese

Shopping List

- elbow macaroni (1 lb)
- cheddar cheese (1 lb or 4 cups)
- Parmesan cheese (3 Tbsp)
- milk (3 cups)
- flour (3 Tbsp)
- butter (3 Tbsp)
- breadcrumbs (3 Tbsp)
- nutmeg

An Easy-Fix Option for this recipe can be downloaded for free at

www.yourkidscooking.net

. . . and to Complete Your Meal

frozen peas
fresh tomatoes

Macaroni and cheese is a good source of dairy, protein, and grains. But half of your plate should be vegetables or fruit, so complete your meal with lots of fresh sliced tomatoes and frozen peas.

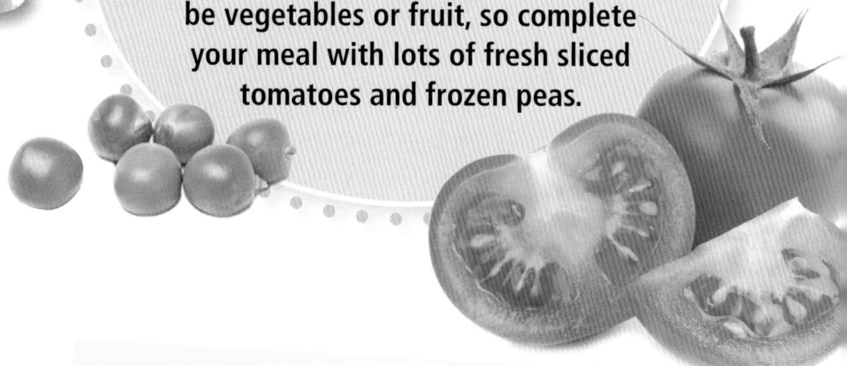

Shopping Tip

You can use all kinds of cheese to make macaroni and cheese, but homemade mac and cheese is usually made with cheddar cheese. Cheddar cheese is available in mild, medium, sharp, and extra-sharp varieties. Mild cheddar has a pleasant milky aroma and creamy texture. Extra-sharp cheddar, which has been aged one year or longer, has a richer flavor and a drier, more crumbly texture.

What's On Your Plate?

Half your grains should be whole grains, so try whole-wheat pasta for added nutrition.

none

pasta

Empty Calories
cheese
whole milk
butter

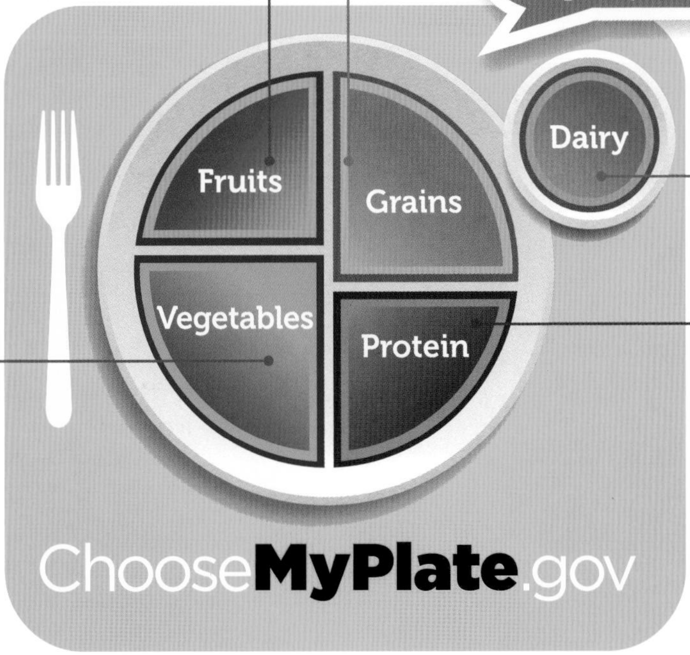

low-fat milk
cheese

cheese
milk

tomatoes
peas

In the Spotlight

Cheese provides high-quality protein needed to stay healthy, but it contains a lot of empty calories, so choose low-fat cheese whenever possible.

Pasta is a good source of grains, but half of the grains you eat should be whole grains. Whole-wheat pasta is a healthy alternative to traditional pasta made with refined white flour because it contains more fiber and protein.

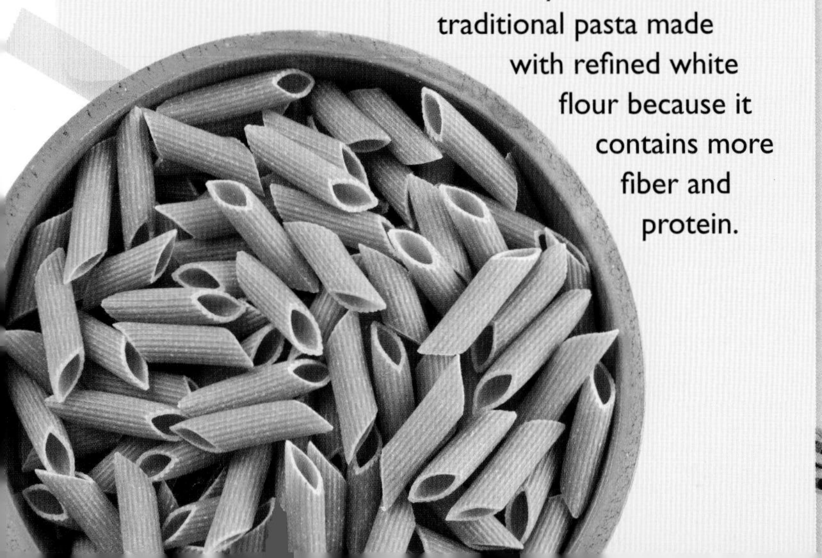

The Skinny on Milk

Skim or 1% reduced-fat milk is an excellent source of calcium which helps maintain strong bones and teeth. Reduced-fat milk contains the same amount of calcium as whole milk making it a healthy alternative.

A healthy diet includes three 8-ounce servings of reduced-fat dairy products a day.

Get Ready!

Start Recipe 2: Macaroni & Cheese before completing this step.

Ingredients

elbow macaroni

cheddar cheese

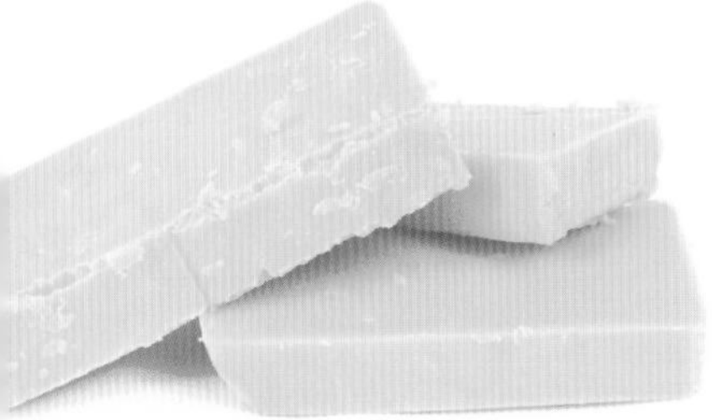

Parmesan cheese

milk

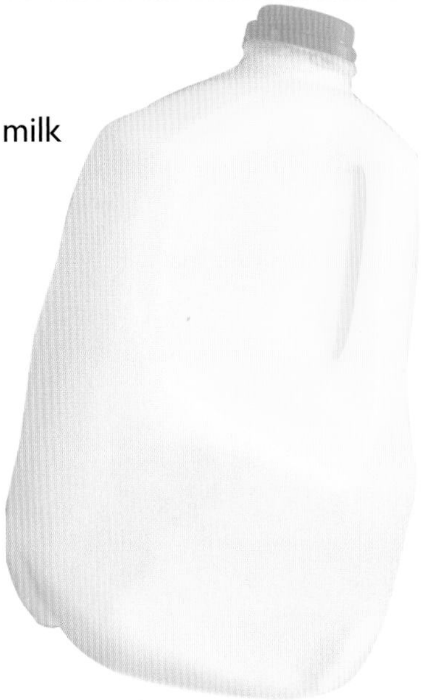

flour

butter

breadcrumbs

nutmeg

Complete Your Meal

frozen peas | fresh tomatoes

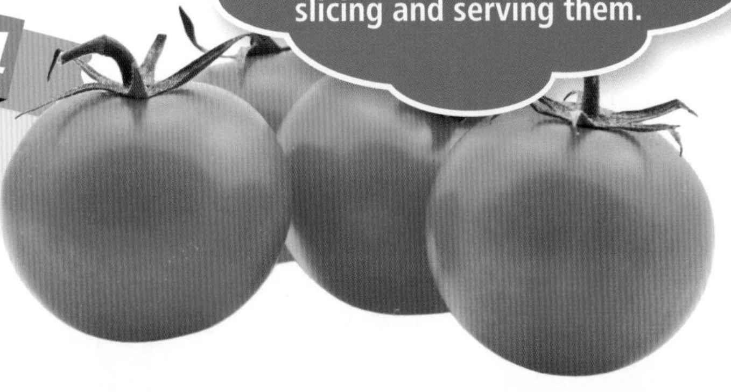

Remember to always wash tomatoes before slicing and serving them.

Utensils

Cookware

stockpot

saucepan *(medium)*

casserole dish *(9 x 13 inches)*

Measurement

measuring spoons

liquid measuring cup *(large)*

straightedge *(optional)*

Tools

cheese grater

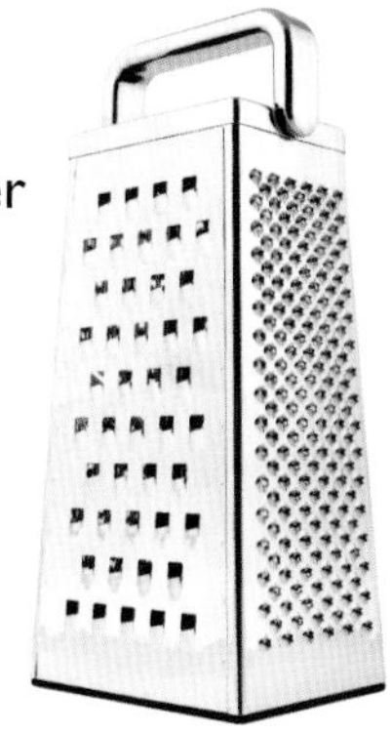

whisk

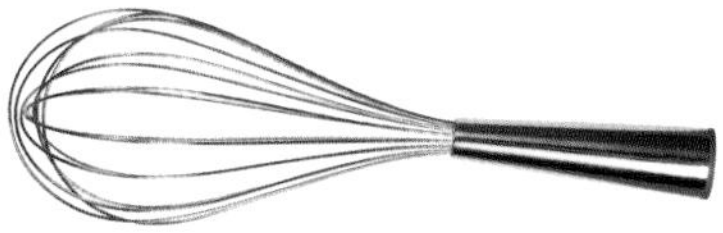

rubber spatula

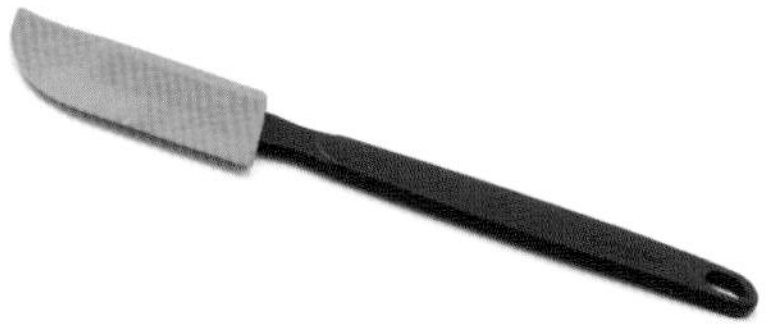

Other

bowls *(2 small)*

colander

cutting board

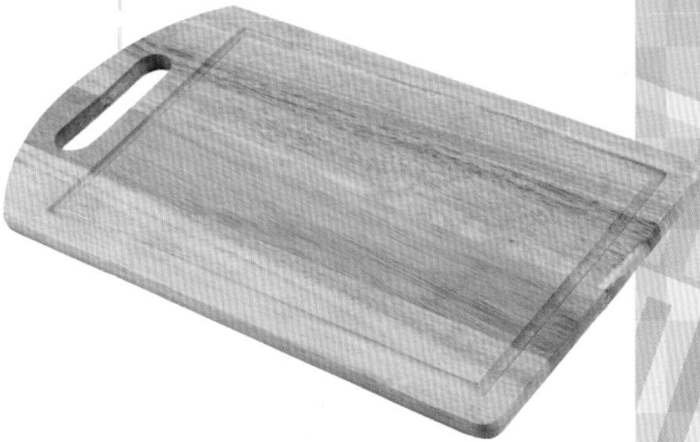

Guess What!

Macaroni and cheese is one of the top ten favorite food choices for kids. Maybe that's why there are two restaurants in New York City that serve only macaroni and cheese and two cookbooks consisting entirely of recipes for this all-time favorite.

Click CONTINUE when you're done!

Get Set!

Watch the *Get Set!* segment before completing these steps.

- fill stockpot $^2/_3$ **full of water**
- turn burner to high heat
- add a **palmful of salt**
- cover pot

1 **Preheat** the pasta water.

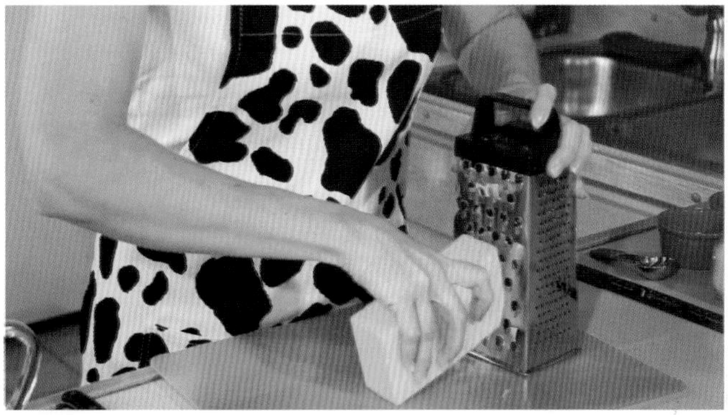

- grate **4 cups cheese**

2 **Grate** the cheese.

- measure **3 Tbsp flour** into a small bowl

3 **Measure** the flour.

A 1-inch piece of butter is about the same as 3 tablespoons.

4 **Measure** the butter.

- cut and set aside
  3 Tbsp butter

5 **Measure** the milk.

- measure **3 cups milk** into a liquid measuring cup

6 **Make** the topping.

- in a small bowl, toss together:
  2 Tbsp breadcrumbs
  2 Tbsp Parmesan cheese

Click CONTINUE when you're done!

Get Cooking!

Watch the *Get Cooking!* segment before completing these steps.

375° Pre-heat

- add **1 lb pasta** to boiling water and stir briefly
- adjust heat to maintain a slow boil
- cover pot and leave a vent for the steam to escape

1 Cook the pasta.

Remember, butter burns easily, so it's best to melt the butter slowly over low heat.

- melt butter over low heat
- add flour; whisk until a smooth paste forms

2 Make the roux.

- add milk to the roux and stir constantly until it begins to simmer
- reduce heat immediately to maintain simmer; continue stirring
- cook until sauce thickens, then turn off burner
- add grated cheese and a dash or two of nutmeg, then stir until cheese melts

3 Make the cheese sauce.

Don't let the milk boil! If it does, it will quickly boil over and make a huge mess.

Make sure you take pictures as you go through the steps!

- drain pasta into a colander
- shake to remove any excess moisture; return to stockpot

4 **Drain** the pasta.

Be efficient and do a little clean up while the casserole is cooking!

- combine pasta and cheese sauce
- pour into casserole dish; sprinkle with breadcrumb topping mixture
- bake uncovered at 375°F for 15 minutes or so

5 **Assemble and bake** the casserole.

Always place hot items on a hot pad or trivet—never directly on the countertop!

- remove the casserole to a hot pad or trivet and let it cool for 5–10 minutes before serving
- plate it up with sliced fresh tomatoes and cooked peas

6 **Plate it up and enjoy!**

Complete Your Meal

Ask your sous chef to slice the tomatoes and cook the peas while the casserole is in the oven.

Happy Eating!

Test Your Skills!

Here's another fun and delicious recipe you can make to practice your new skills.

SERVES:
6–8

KITCHEN TIME:
20 min

READY TO SERVE:
35 min

Baked Penne with Bacon and Peas

Get Ready!

Ingredients

penne pasta *(1 lb)*

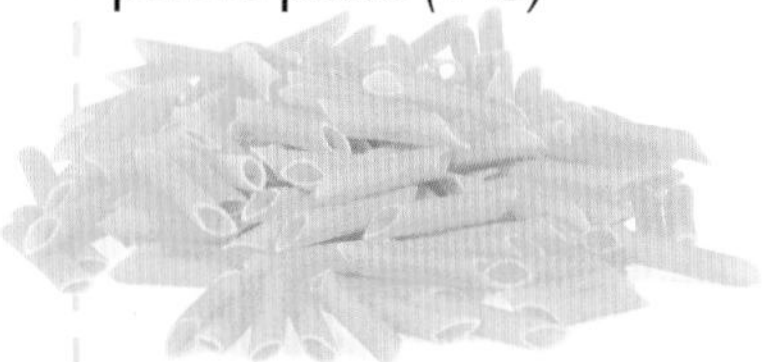

real bacon bits *(1 4-oz pkg)*

frozen peas *(1 cup)*

flour

milk *(4 cups)*

butter

grated Parmesan cheese *(3 Tbsp)*

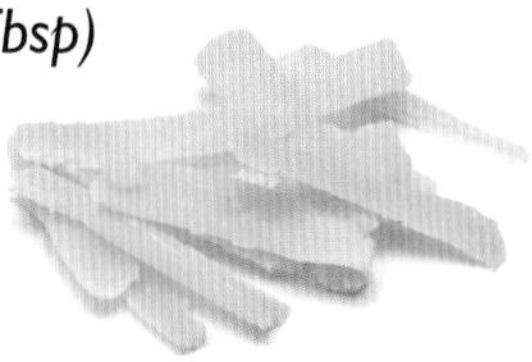

breadcrumbs *(3 Tbsp)*

nutmeg

OPTIONAL

salad kit *(1 bag)*

baguette

Utensils

COOKWARE

stockpot

saucepan *(large)*

casserole dish *(9 x 13 inches)*

TOOLS

whisk
rubber spatula

MEASUREMENT

liquid measuring cup *(large)*
measuring cups
measuring spoons

OTHER

colander
bowls *(2 small, 1 medium)*
catch-all

STACK UP YOUR KNOWLEDGE

Don't forget to check off the STACK items you mastered on page 142.

Get Set!

1 Measure ingredients for the sauce.

- measure 4 cups milk into liquid measuring cup
- measure 3 Tbsp flour into small bowl
- cut and set aside 3 Tbsp butter

2 Measure ingredients for the pasta.

- into medium bowl, measure:
  1 cup frozen peas
  ½ cup bacon bits

3 Prepare pasta water.

- heat stockpot filled $^2/_3$ full of water on high heat
- add palmful of salt
- cover pot

4 Prepare topping.

- in small bowl, toss together:
  3 Tbsp Parmesan cheese
  3 Tbsp breadcrumbs

Get Cooking!

Don't forget to vent the lid to prevent boiling over.

375° Pre-heat

1 Cook the pasta.

- cook pasta 2 minutes less than indicated on package

2 Make the roux.

- melt butter
- add flour; whisk until smooth paste forms

3 Make the Béchamel sauce.

- add milk and **1 tsp salt** to roux; stir until sauce begins to simmer
- reduce heat to maintain simmer
- cook until sauce thickens, stirring occasionally
- add **¼ tsp nutmeg**

4 Drain the pasta.

- drain pasta into a colander
- return pasta to stockpot

5 Assemble and bake the casserole.

- add Béchamel sauce, bacon bits, and peas to pasta
- stir to combine
- pour pasta into casserole dish; top with breadcrumb mixture
- bake for 15–20 minutes at 375°F

6 Plate it up and enjoy!

- serve pasta with a green salad and sliced baguette

Puppy Chow

It may be called "puppy chow," but this tasty treat is way too yummy to share with our furry little friends! This cereal snack is quick and easy to make and it's perfect for a lunch-box treat. But pack a little extra . . . you may have to share it with all your friends!

What You'll Need

- 1 cup chocolate chips
- ¼ cup butter
- 1 cup peanut butter
- 1 box Crispix cereal
- 2 cups powdered sugar

You can use any cereal that is similar to Crispix. Use a whole-grain cereal to make it a healthier snack.

What You'll Do

1. Melt chocolate chips, peanut butter and butter over low heat.
2. Put cereal in a large bowl and stir in chocolate mixture. Mix together well.
3. Put 1 cup powdered sugar in a large brown paper bag, then add cereal mixture and the rest of the powdered sugar.
4. Shake well until all the cereal is covered.
5. Store in an airtight container.

Expand Your Horizons!

Practice everything you've learned so far by making one or all of these delicious recipes.

Fettuccini Alfredo
Cheese Lasagna
Creamy Pesto Pasta
Baked Rigatoni with Béchamel Sauce
Shrimp with Mornay Sauce
Parmesan and Butter Noodles
Cheese Fondue
Nacho Cheese Sauce
Bread Pudding
Bananas Foster French Toast

The recipes above, and many more, are available for download at

www.yourkidscooking.net

Tell a Friend!

Ask your sous chef to post pictures and a funny story about your cooking experience on our Facebook page and to keep their social media sites updated on all the fun you're having!

LESSON 3

Tamale Pie

SERVES: 6–8

COMPLETE THE LESSON: 40 min

READY TO SERVE: 1 hr 30 min

A Lunch-line Favorite

In this lesson you're going to make another quick and delicious casserole called tamale pie, which is an American dish based on a traditional Latin American favorite, the tamale. If you've never heard of tamale pie, ask your grandparents about it, because back in the 50s and 60s tamale pie was a favorite in school cafeterias all over the country!

Get Prepared!

Here's a little Sneak Peek of how this recipe is made.

Note to the Chef

In this lesson you are going to learn one of the most important cooking skills there is—how to use a knife. Using a knife is a big responsibility so you'll want to pay close attention. And be sure to watch the "Knife Safety" segment on the DVD and read the Sharp Stuff safety tips on page xxvi. And remember—never use a knife without the permission or supervision of your sous chef!

1. **Make** a ground beef filling.

2. **Pour** the filling into a casserole dish and top with cheese.

STACK UP YOUR KNOWLEDGE

Here's what you'll learn in this lesson.

SKILLS

- ☐ chop onions
- ☐ brown ground beef
- ☐ use a knife safely
- ☐ open cans

TERMS

- ☐ brown
- ☐ chop
- ☐ bench scraper

A

3 **Cover** casserole with cornmeal crust.

4 **Bake** for 45 minutes.

Note to the Sous Chef

Tamale pie is surprisingly simple to make and presents no particular challenges except to the youngest of chefs. However, since this recipe requires chefs to use a knife, it is important for the sous chef to be present at all times, supervising and providing guidance as the young chef learns and practices these new knife skills. It is highly recommended that you, as the sous chef, model the techniques first. If you feel your child is not ready, complete those steps that require the use of a knife yourself.

Cooking Know-How

- ☐ browning meat
- ☐ kitchen safety *(using a knife)*
- ☐ cooking onions
- ☐ baking casseroles

Get Prepared!

When you're ready to start cooking, watch *Recipe 3: Tamale Pie.*

What You'll Need

. . . to make Tamale Pie

Shopping List

- ground beef (1 lb)
- cheddar cheese (1/2 lb or 2 cups)
- cornmeal (1 1/2 cups)
- onion (1 medium)
- corn (1 15-oz can or 2 cups frozen)
- olives (1 15-oz can)
- tomato sauce (1 15-oz can)
- chili powder
- butter (1–2 Tbsp)
- diced green chili peppers (1 4-oz can, optional)

An Easy-Fix Option for this recipe can be downloaded for free at

www.yourkidscooking.net

You'll want to use yellow cornmeal, not white.

. . . and to Complete Your Meal

coleslaw mix
bell peppers *(any colors)*

Tamale pie is a good source of protein, but it should be served with fresh vegetables to be nutritionally complete. We suggest coleslaw and fresh sliced bell peppers to complete this south-of-the-border meal.

Chiles come in mild, medium, and hot, so be sure to check the label so you don't bring home the wrong kind!

Shopping Tip

Here are some guidelines for choosing the right variety of ground beef:

- The maximum fat allowed in ground beef is 30% (making it 70% lean)—which is a high fat content.
- The best choice is "extra lean" which contains no more than 5% fat (95% lean).
- Ground chuck has the highest fat in ground beef cuts. Ground sirloin has the least.
- The lower the fat content, the less flavorful the meat. Lean or extra-lean ground beef is fine for a recipe made with lots of other ingredients and flavorings.

What's On Your Plate?

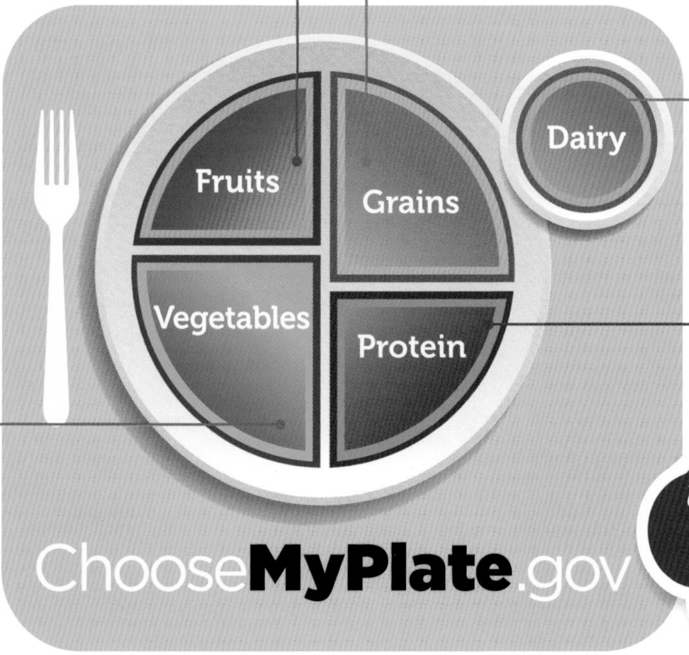

Fruits: none

Grains: cornmeal, corn

Dairy: none

Protein: cheese, ground beef

Vegetables: olives, tomato sauce, onions, bell peppers, cabbage

Empty Calories: ground beef, cheese, butter

Use lean or extra-lean ground beef to reduce the amount of fat and empty calories.

IN THE Spotlight

Ground beef is a good source of quality protein but can be high in fat and cholesterol. Choose lean or extra-lean varieties to reduce the amount of empty calories. See "Shopping Tip" on page 32 for more information on buying ground beef.

Corn is a whole grain and a good source of carbohydrates, but it offers little in the way of nutrition. Cornmeal is made from ground corn. You can buy whole-grain cornmeal, but cornmeal has usually been degerminated and is not a whole-grain product.

Whole-Grain or Not?

Any food made from wheat, rice, oats, cornmeal, or other cereal grain is a grain product. Not all grain products, however, are made from whole grains. Check the ingredient list on food packaging and choose foods that have a whole-grain ingredient listed first on the list. Words like "whole wheat," "brown rice," whole-grain cornmeal," "whole rye", or "oatmeal" indicate a whole-grain ingredient.

Get Ready!

Start Recipe 3: Tamale Pie before completing this step.

Ingredients

ground beef

cheddar cheese

cornmeal

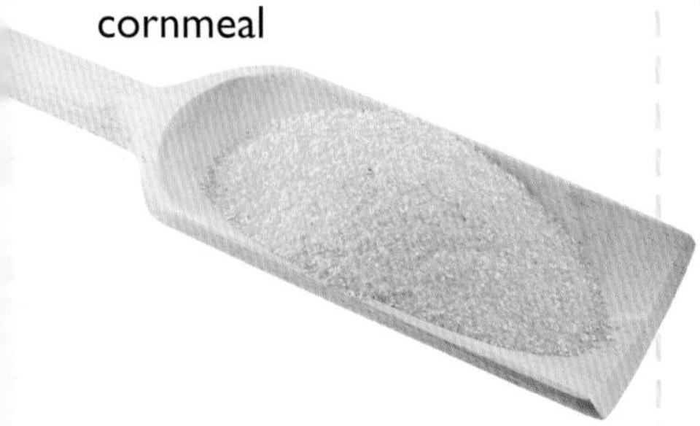

onion *(1)*

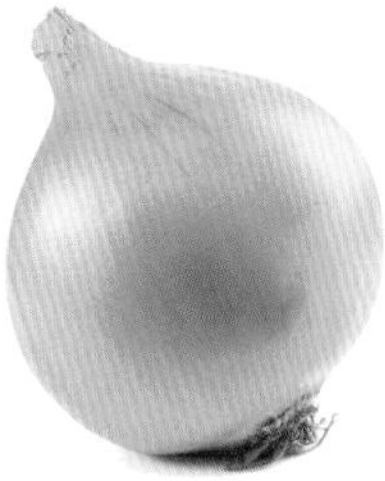

corn

olives *(1 can)*

tomato sauce *(1 can)*

chili powder

butter

diced green chiles *(optional)*

Complete Your Meal

coleslaw mix | bell peppers

Utensils

Cookware

saucepan *(medium)*

sauté pan *(large)*

casserole dish *(10 x 10 inches)*

Measurement

measuring cups

measuring spoons

liquid measuring cup *(large)*

straightedge *(optional)*

Tools

can opener

chef's knife

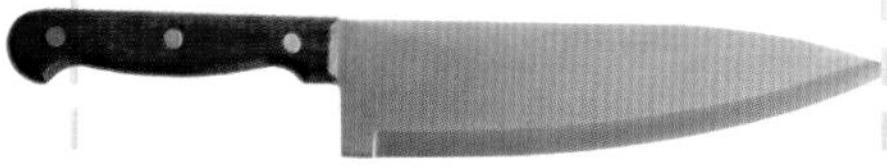

flat spatula

whisk

rubber spatula

cheese grater

bench scraper

Other

bowls *(2 medium, 2 small)*

colander

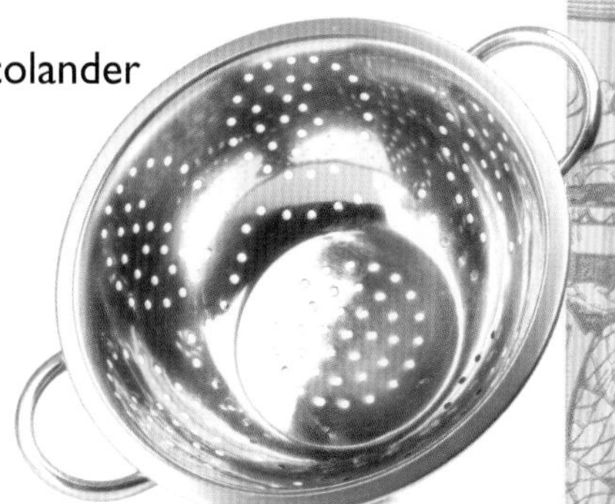

cutting board

catch-all

Click CONTINUE when you're done!

Get Set!

Watch the *Get Set!* segment before completing these steps.

1 **Grate** the cheese.

- grate **2 cups cheese** into medium bowl

2 **Measure** the cornmeal.

- measure **1 ½ cups cornmeal** into medium bowl

3 **Prepare** water for the cornmeal crust.

- measure **4 cups water** into medium saucepan
- cut and set aside **2 Tbsp butter**

4 Chop the onion.

- cut the stem and root ends off the onion
- cut onion in half from top to bottom
- remove papery outer skin
- cut into ¼-inch slices
- turn slices 90° and cut ¼-inch slices in the opposite direction
- transfer chopped pieces to small bowl using your bench scraper

5 Open the canned items.

- open and drain the corn and chiles; place in small bowl
- open and drain the olives; leave in colander
- open the tomato sauce; set aside until later

6 Chop the olives.

- leave 10–12 olives in colander; split each olive in half
- chop remaining olives into small pieces; add to bowl of corn

Click CONTINUE when you're done!

Get Cooking!

Watch the *Get Cooking!* segment before completing these steps.

375° Pre-heat

1 Brown the ground beef.

- cook **1 lb ground beef** over medium heat
- use flat spatula to break beef into small pieces while cooking
- begin heating water on medium-high heat

2 Cook the onions (and chiles).

- as soon as beef is broken into small pieces, add onions (and chiles, if desired)
- cook 5–7 minutes or until onions begin to soften and turn clear and there is no sign of pink, uncooked beef

3 Finish cooking the filling.

- to the ground beef, add:
  - **corn**
  - **chopped olives**
  - **tomato sauce**
  - **2 tsp salt**
  - **2–3 tsp chili powder**
- stir ingredients together
- adjust heat to maintain a simmer; let sauce cook uncovered for 15–20 minutes, or until thickened

Remember to clean up the kitchen and wash dishes while the casserole is cooking!

Make sure you take pictures as you go through the steps!

Complete Your Meal

Ask your sous chef to prepare the coleslaw and peppers while the casserole is in the oven.

4 Assemble the casserole.

- pour filling into casserole dish
- sprinkle grated cheese evenly over filling

5 Cook the cornmeal crust.

- add cornmeal slowly and gradually to cold water, stirring continuously
- add **1 tsp salt** to taste
- bring to boil; reduce heat to maintain slow boil
- cook, stirring continuously, about 5 minutes or until cornmeal is about as thick as applesauce; turn off burner and remove from heat
- stir in **1–2 Tbsp butter** until it melts

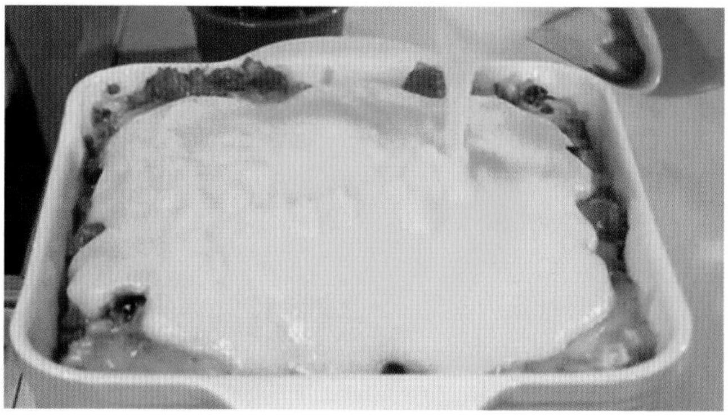

6 Add the cornmeal crust and bake.

- pour cornmeal crust evenly over filling
- leave opening around the edges for heat to escape
- arrange reserved olives on crust
- bake at 375°F for about 45 minutes

7 Plate it up and enjoy!

- let the casserole cool for 10–15 minutes before serving
- serve with sliced bell peppers and coleslaw

Happy Eating!

Test Your Skills!

Here's another fun and delicious recipe you can make to practice your new skills.

SERVES:
6–8

KITCHEN TIME:
15–20 min

READY TO SERVE:
1 hr 20 min

Chili with Cheesy Cornbread Muffins

Get Ready!

Ingredients

kidney beans *(1 15-oz can)*

black beans *(1 15-oz can)*

pinto beans *(1 15-oz can)*

diced tomatoes *(1 15-oz can)*

tomato sauce *(1 15-oz can)*

ground beef *(1 lb extra-lean)*

onion *(1 medium)*

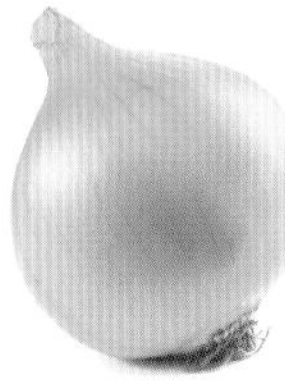

chili powder

sugar

crushed cayenne pepper *(optional)*

cornmeal muffin mix

Check the package for additional ingredients you may need, such as eggs.

cheddar cheese *(½ cup grated)*

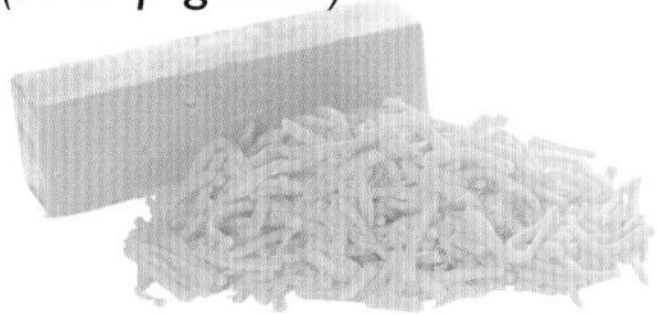

corn *(½ cup frozen)*

sour cream *(optional)*

OPTIONAL
green salad or coleslaw

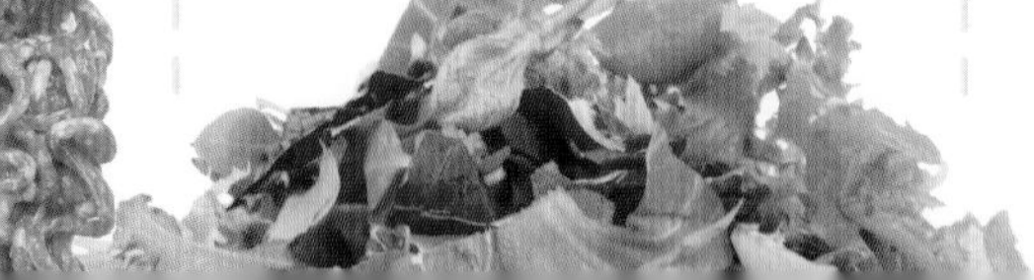

Utensils

COOKWARE
stockpot

muffin tin

TOOLS
flat spatula
rubber spatula
chef's knife
wooden spoon
can opener

MEASUREMENT
measuring cups
measuring spoons

OTHER
cutting board
muffin cup liners
bowls *(2 small, 1 medium)*
catch-all

Tamale Pie

STACK UP YOUR KNOWLEDGE

Don't forget to check off the STACK items you mastered on page 142.

Get Set!

1 Chop the onion.

- chop 1 onion into ½-inch pieces

2 Open canned items.

- open all the canned items; do not drain

3 Grate the cheese.

- grate ½ cup cheddar cheese into a small bowl

4 Prepare muffin mix.

- prepare muffins according to directions on package
- stir corn and grated cheese into muffin mix
- spoon mix into muffin cups according to directions on package
- preheat oven according to directions on package

Wait to bake the muffins until the chili is about half-way done cooking.

Get Cooking!

1 Cook the onions and ground beef.

- heat 1–2 Tbsp oil in the stockpot over medium heat
- when oil is hot, add the onion; cook until they begin to soften
- add ground beef and cook until browned on the outside

2 Finish and cook the chili.

- to the stockpot, add all the canned items and the ingredients below:
  - 2 Tbsp sugar
  - 3 tsp chili powder
  - 1 ½ tsp salt
  - ½ tsp pepper
  - ¼ tsp crushed cayenne pepper *(optional)*
- bring the chili to a boil; reduce heat to low, cover and simmer for about 1 hour

3 Bake the cornbread muffins.

- bake muffins according to directions on package

4 Plate it up and enjoy!

- garnish with grated cheddar cheese and/or sour cream *(optional)*
- serve with cornbread muffins hot out of the oven

Peachy Popsicles

These refreshing popsicles are super easy to make and are a super tasty way to include more fruit in your diet! And if you're not crazy about peaches, try substituting frozen mangos or berries.

What You'll Need

- 1 15-oz can peaches
- 1 ¼ cups orange juice
- 1 Tbsp powdered sugar
- ½ cup canned fruit salad, drained

Make sure you have popsicle molds and sticks before getting started!

What You'll Do

1. Blend the peaches, orange juice, and powdered sugar until smooth and frothy.
2. Spoon half of the fruit salad into the 4 molds.
3. Fill each mold half full with the juice.
4. Add the rest of the fruit salad.
5. Add more juice to top off each mold.
6. Insert a stick into each mold and freeze for at least 8 hours.

For a creamier popsicle, try adding ½ cup of yogurt.

Allow popsicles to soften a bit before eating.

Expand Your Horizons!

Practice everything you've learned so far making any of these recipes!

Sloppy Joes
Classic Lasagna
Beef Quesadilla
Cheesy Chili Mac
Tuna Noodle Casserole
Beefy Cheese Nachos
Sausage and Veggie Frittata
Beef Enchilada Casserole
Ground Beef Stroganoff
Breakfast Burrito

The recipes above, and many more, are available for download at

www.yourkidscooking.net

Tell a Friend!

Pretend you're a restaurant critic and write a review of your latest cooking triumph. Then ask your sous chef to post your review on Twitter and Facebook.

LESSON 4

Quiche

SERVES: 6–8

COMPLETE THE LESSON: 40 min

READY TO SERVE: 1 hr 30 min

More Pie, Anyone?

In this lesson you're going to learn how to make another kind of pie—one that can be served at any meal . . . except dessert! It's called quiche, and it's a savory, open-faced pastry-crust pie baked with a filling of eggs, cheese, meat and vegetables. It's a whole meal in one pie crust—and it's deeeelicious!

Get Prepared!

Here's a little Sneak Peek of how this recipe is made.

Note to the Chef

I hope you're excited about this lesson because you are going to learn how to make a pie crust from scratch and that is something to be proud of! Many people think homemade pie crust is really complicated and hard to make. Balderdash! Making pie crust is quick and easy and fun! It might take a few tries to make the perfect crust, but practice makes perfect, so let's start practicing!

1. **Make** a pie crust.

2. **Fill** crust with cooked bacon, spinach and onions.

STACK UP YOUR KNOWLEDGE

Here's what you'll learn in this lesson.

SKILLS

- ☐ use a pastry blender
- ☐ roll out a pie crust

TERMS

- ☐ cutting in
- ☐ pastry blender
- ☐ rolling pin

A

3 **Top** with grated cheese and custard filling.

4 **Bake** for 45 minutes.

Note to the Sous Chef

In this lesson, your young chef will learn the art of making a homemade pie crust. Though it may seem complicated, homemade pie crust is really quite quick and easy to make. That being said, it does take some practice to get a nice, flakey crust, so don't worry if this first attempt doesn't turn out perfectly. Practice makes perfect and once they get the hang of it, it's as easy as . . . well . . . pie!

Cooking Know-How

- ☐ making a pie crust
- ☐ cooking bacon
- ☐ cooking spinach
- ☐ testing for doneness
- ☐ kitchen safety *(handling raw meat)*

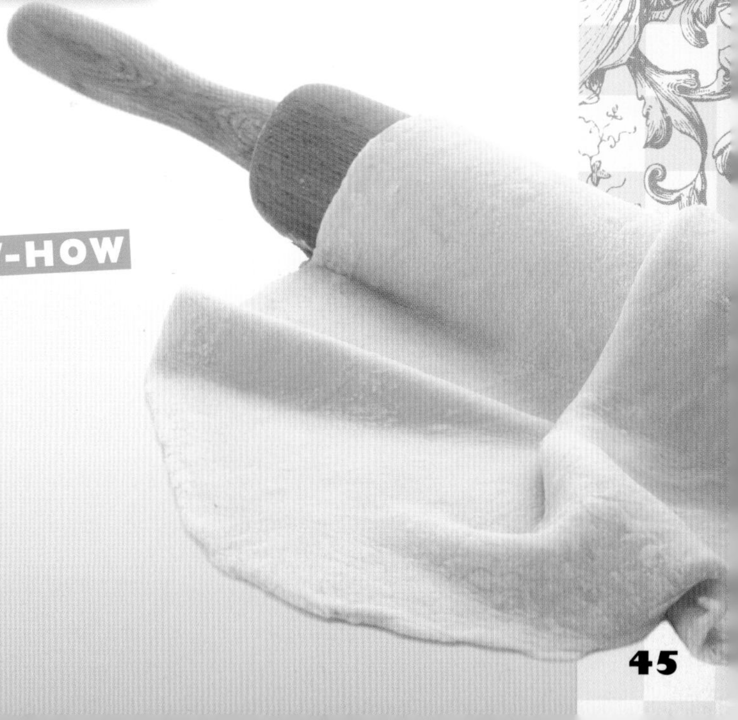

Get Prepared!

When you're ready to start cooking, watch *Recipe 4: Quiche.*

What You'll Need

. . . to make Quiche

Shopping List

- flour
- shortening ($1/3$ cup)
- spinach (1 lb fresh)
- onion (1 medium)
- Swiss or Gruyère cheese ($1/2$ lb)
- eggs (6 large)
- cream (2 cups)
- nutmeg
- bacon (6 slices)

An Easy-Fix Option for this recipe can be downloaded for free at

www.yourkidscooking.net

. . . and to

Complete Your Meal

frozen hash browns
fresh fruit | fruit juice

Quiche is a good source of protein and dairy, but it should be served with fruit or vegetables to make it a more balanced meal. Hash browns or fried potatoes make delicious side dishes, too!

Shopping Tip

Frozen spinach is not recommended because it is time-consuming to thaw it out and remove the excess water it contains. Fresh spinach is much better to use in quiche. Buy "triple-washed" spinach and you won't even need to wash it first!

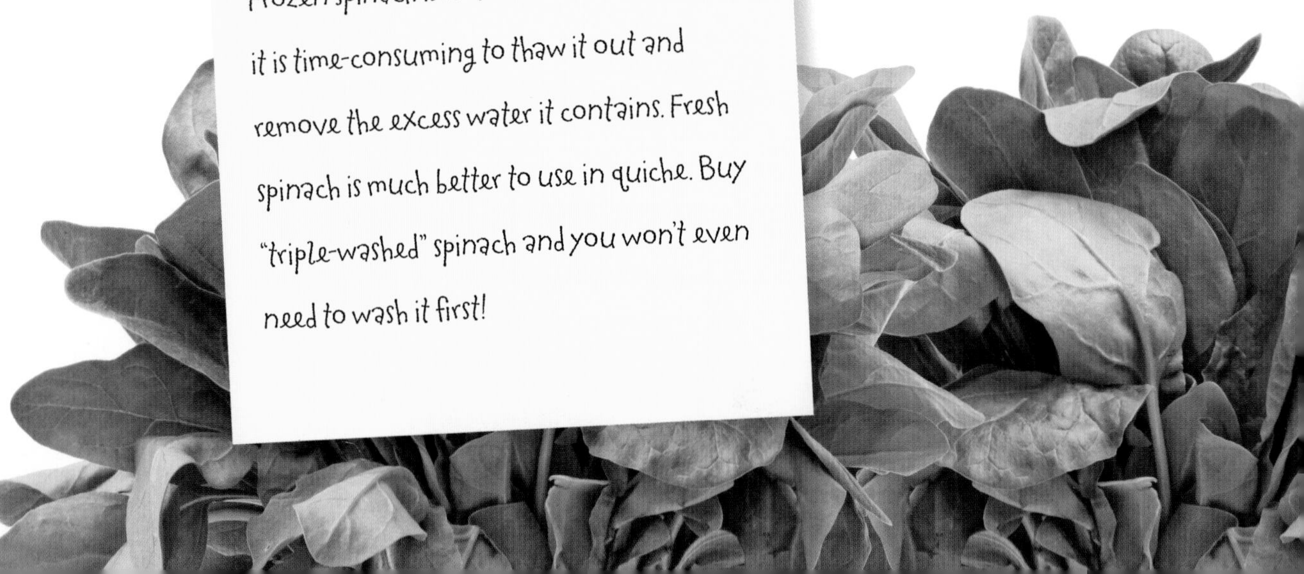

What's On Your Plate?

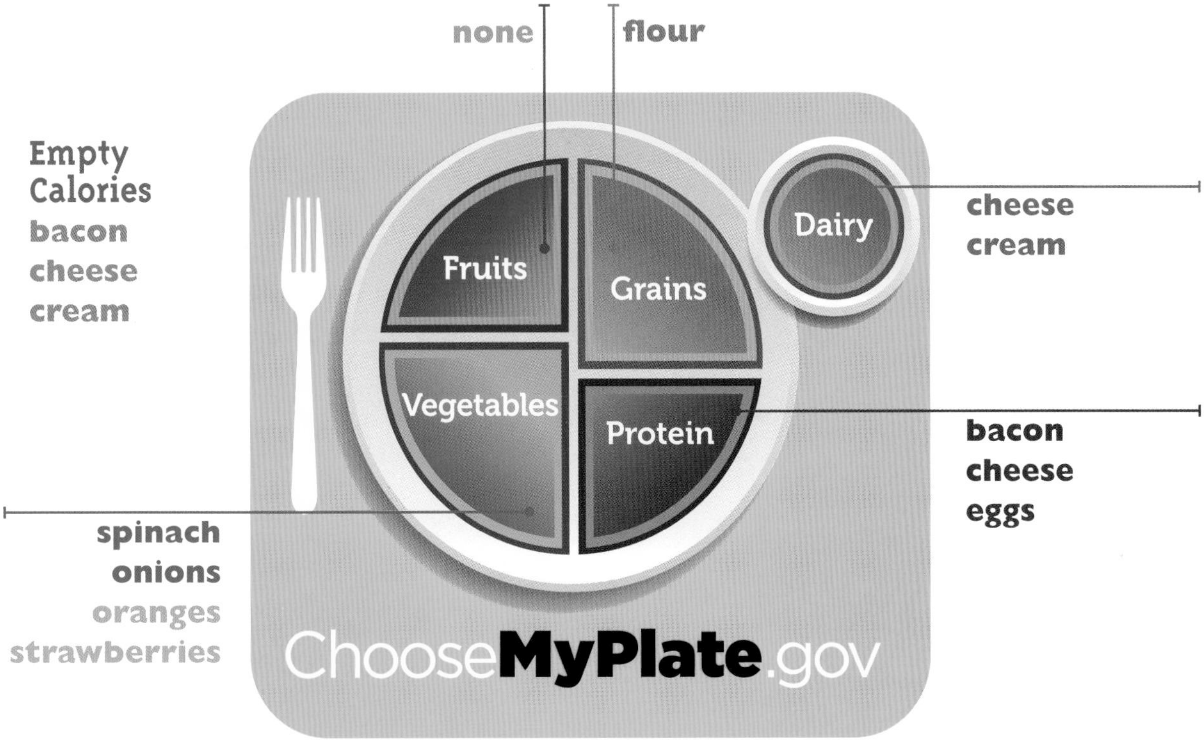

IN THE Spotlight

Spinach is chock-full of iron, vitamin C and all sorts of other important nutrients. Including spinach in your meals will help you get many of the vitamins and minerals you need for a healthy body. Spinach can be added raw to a salad or sautéed and added to casseroles, rice dishes or even scrambled eggs. However you eat it, it will be good for you!

Bacon is a good source of protein but it is also very high in saturated fat and empty calories (almost 75% of the calories in bacon come from fat). Limit your consumption or choose leaner varieties of bacon made from turkey or soy. Read and compare nutrition labels though—bacon made with turkey is not always the healthier choice!

Solid Fats and Empty Calories

Most of the calories found in cheese, bacon, and cream come from solid fats and are considered empty calories. And if you remember, it's important not to eat too many of those! To reduce the amount of empty calories in your diet, eat foods like cheese, bacon, and cream less often or decrease the amount you eat.

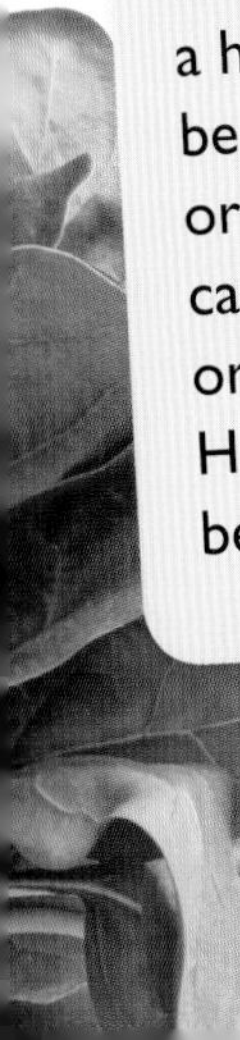

Get Ready!

Start *Recipe 4: Quiche* before completing this step.

Ingredients

flour

shortening

spinach *(1 lb fresh)*

onion *(1 medium)*

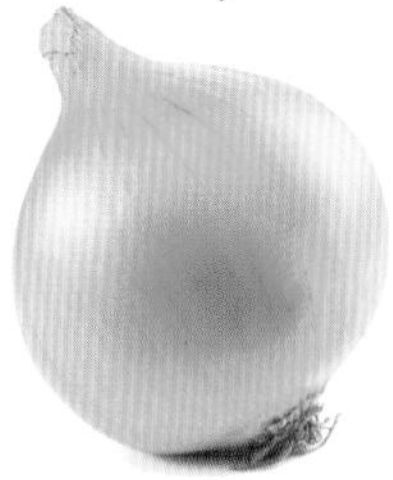

Swiss or Gruyère cheese

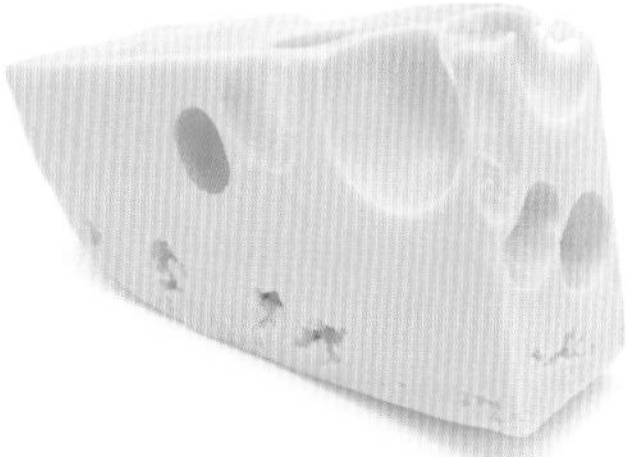

eggs *(6)*

cream

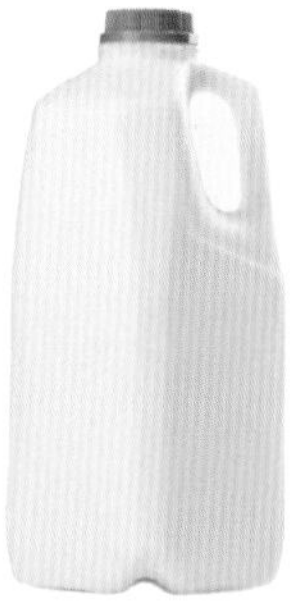

nutmeg

bacon *(6 slices)*

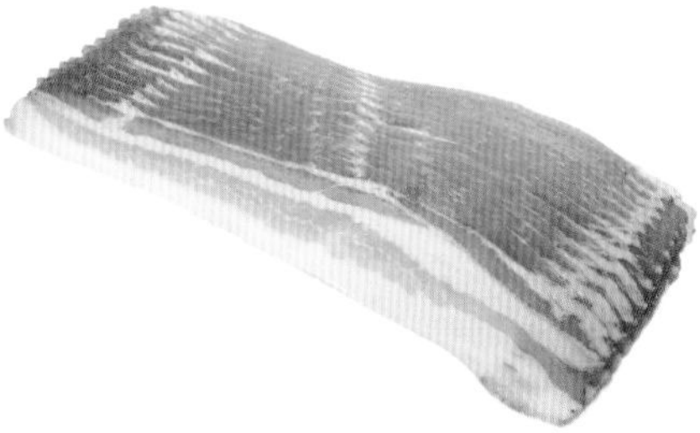

Complete Your Meal

frozen hash browns
fresh fruit | fruit juice

Utensils

Cookware

pie plate *(9-inch diameter)*

frying pan *(large)*

Measurement

measuring cups

measuring spoons

liquid measuring cup *(large)*

straightedge *(optional)*

Tools

rolling pin

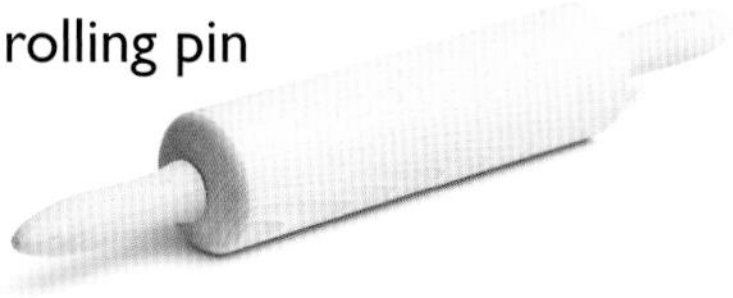

pastry blender

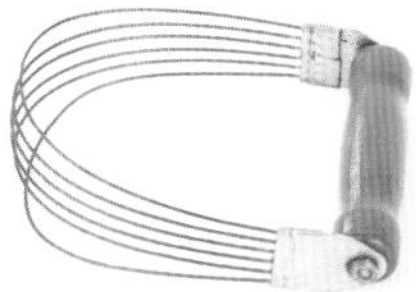

flat spatula

cheese grater

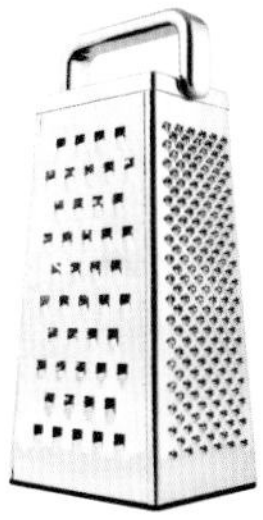

whisk

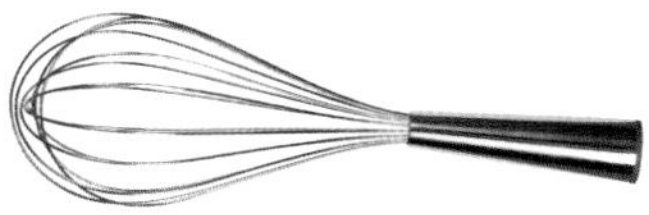

chef's knife

bench scraper

Other

bowls *(3 small, 3 medium, 1 large)*

glass bowl *(small, for bacon grease)*

plastic wrap

cutting board(s)

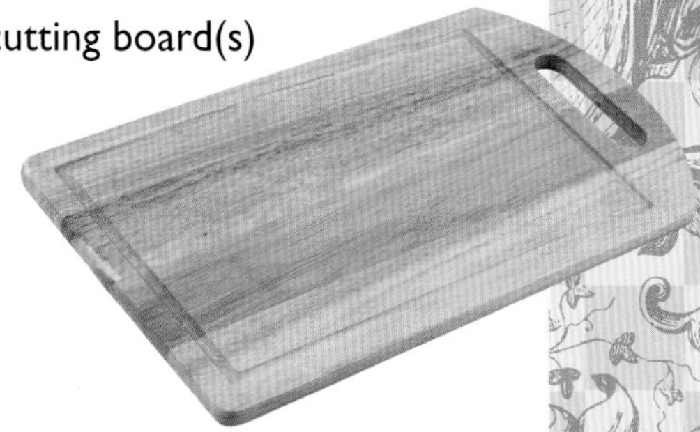

catch-all

Click CONTINUE when you're done!

Get Set!

Watch the *Get Set!* segment before completing these steps.

1 **Make** the pie crust dough.

- into medium bowl, measure:
  - **1 ½ cups flour**
  - **⅓ cup shortening**
  - **1 tsp salt**
- cut shortening into the flour
- add **1–2 Tbsp water** at a time, until the dough sticks together in a ball
- form into a disc; wrap in plastic
- chill 10–15 minutes

This is the most important part of making the dough. It should be moist enough to stick together in a ball but not so moist that it sticks to your hands.

2 **Chop** the spinach.

- rough-chop the spinach; transfer to large bowl

3 **Chop** the onion.

- chop onion into ¼-inch pieces; transfer to small bowl

4 **Grate** the cheese.

- grate **2 cups cheese;** transfer to medium bowl

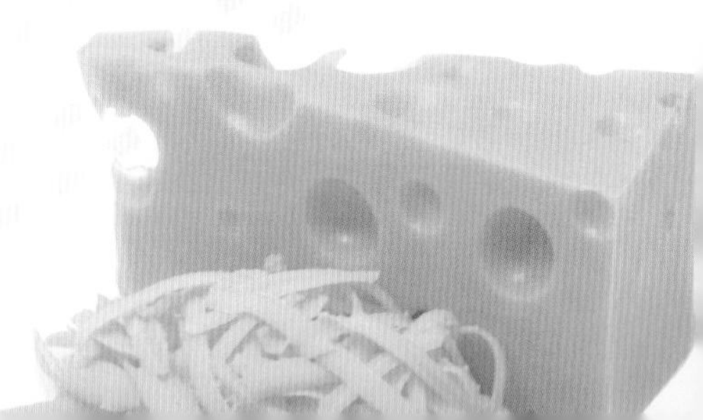

• in medium bowl, whisk:

6 eggs
2 cups cream
1 tsp salt
¼ tsp nutmeg

5 Make the custard filling.

• spread a little flour on rolling surface and rolling pin
• roll dough into about a 13-inch circle
• roll crust onto your rolling pin
• unroll crust into pie plate
• pinch extra dough around edges to form a thick outer rim

6 **Roll** out the pie crust.

Remember to wash your hands after handling the bacon!

• chop bacon into ½-inch pieces
• transfer to small bowl

7 **Chop** up the bacon.

Click CONTINUE when you're done!

Get Cooking!

Watch the *Get Cooking!* segment before completing these steps.

1 Fry the bacon.

325° Pre-heat

- cook bacon over medium-high heat until brown and crispy
- remove cooked bacon; blot on paper towel
- pour bacon grease into small glass bowl to cool
- return frying pan to the burner

Do not pour hot bacon grease down the drain because it can clog the pipes.

2 Cook the onions and spinach.

- cook onions until they soften, turn clear and start to brown around edges
- add spinach gradually; cook until wilted and moisture has been cooked off

3 Assemble the quiche.

- fill pie crust with bacon, spinach and onions, and cheese
- pour custard into pie to within ½ inch from top of crust

- bake uncovered at 325°F for 45 minutes or until a knife inserted in the center comes out clean

4 **Bake** the quiche.

You and your sous chef may want to wash up the dishes while the quiche cooks!

- let the quiche cool 15–20 minutes before serving
- serve with fresh fruit, hash browns, and fruit juice

5 **Plate it up and enjoy!**

Complete Your Meal

Ask your sous chef to help you prepare the hash browns and fresh fruit while the quiche is cooling.

Happy Eating!

Test Your Skills!

Here's another fun and delicious recipe you can make to practice your new skills.

SERVES:
6–8

KITCHEN TIME:
30 min

READY TO SERVE:
1 hr 10 min

Chicken Pot Pie

Get Ready!

Ingredients

flour

shortening (*2/3 cup*)

chicken broth (*1 cup*)

milk (*¾ cup*)

onion (*1 medium*)

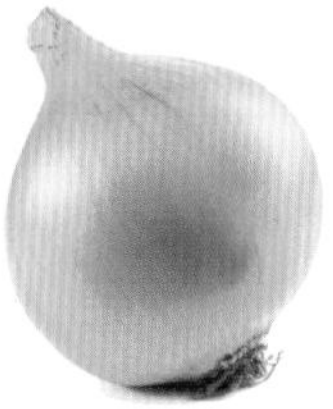

precooked chicken breast
(*1 16-oz package*)

frozen mixed veggies
(*2 cups*)

butter

thyme

OPTIONAL

green salad

Utensils

COOKWARE

pie plate (*9-inch diameter*)
saucepan (*medium*)

TOOLS

rolling pin
pastry blender
cheese grater
chef's knife
whisk
wooden spoon

MEASUREMENT

liquid measuring cup
measuring cups
measuring spoons

OTHER

bowls (*1 small, 2 medium*)
cutting board

STACK UP YOUR KNOWLEDGE

Don't forget to check off the STACK items you mastered on page 142.

Get Set!

1 Make the pie crust dough.

- into medium bowl, measure:
  - 2 ½ cups flour
  - ⅔ cup shortening
  - 1 ½ tsp salt
- cut shortening into flour
- blend in water, a tablespoon or two at a time, until dough is just moist enough to stick together in a ball
- form dough into two discs; wrap in plastic and chill in refrigerator 10–15 minutes
- roll one disc of chilled dough into a 13-inch diameter circle; roll the other into an 11-inch diameter circle; place the larger crust into greased pie plate

2 Measure ingredients for gravy.

425° Pre-heat

- measure and set aside:
  - 3 Tbsp butter
  - 3 Tbsp flour
- into a 2-cup liquid measuring cup, measure:
  - 1 cup chicken broth
  - ¾ cup milk

Add the chicken broth first, then fill with milk to the 1 ¾ cup mark because 1 cup + ¾ cup = 1 ¾ cups.

3 Prepare the chicken.

- chop cooked chicken breast into ½-inch pieces; transfer to medium bowl

4 Prepare the veggies.

- chop onion into ¼-inch pieces; add to chicken
- add frozen vegetables to bowl with chicken and onions; stir to combine

Get Cooking!

1 Make the gravy.

- in large saucepan, make a roux using butter and flour
- add broth and milk; cook until mixture thickens, stirring frequently
- add 1 tsp thyme and salt and pepper to taste

2 Assemble and bake the pie.

- add gravy to bowl with chicken and veggies; stir to combine
- pour filling into pie crust
- top with second crust; trim excess crust and crimp edges together
- cut 8–10 slits in top crust for steam to escape while cooking
- bake at 425° for 30–40 minutes until crust is golden brown and the filling bubbles

3 Plate it up and enjoy!

- let pie cool for 10 minutes
- plate it up and enjoy with a fresh green salad!

Reward Yourself!

Strawberry Shortcake

Here's a delicious way to enjoy fresh strawberries. You can use frozen strawberries if fresh ones are not available. Or try other berries that are in season like raspberries or blackberries or a combination of all three. Anything goes when you're the chef!

What You'll Need

SHORTCAKE

- 2 1/3 cups baking mix
- 2/3 cup milk
- 3 Tbsp sugar
- 3 Tbsp butter, melted

TOPPING

- 4–6 cups sliced strawberries
- ½ cup sugar
- 1 can whipped cream

Instead of using whipped cream, try pouring plain, unwhipped heavy cream over the top. It's delish!

What You'll Do

1. Preheat oven to 425°F.
2. Mix strawberries and sugar.
3. Combine baking mix, sugar and butter.
4. Place 6 large mounds of dough on an ungreased baking sheet.
5. Bake 10–12 minutes or until golden brown.
6. Divide warm shortcake in half; top with berries and whipped cream.

Expand Your Horizons!

Practice everything you've learned so far making any of these recipes!

Italian Stuffed Shells
Fettuccini Carbonara
Calzone
Beef and Potato Pasties
Black Bean Tostadas
Chili Egg Puff Breakfast Casserole
Joe's Special Breakfast Scramble
Pumpkin Pie
Banana Cream Pie
Stella's Raspberry Danish

The recipes above, and many more, are available for download at

www.yourkidscooking.net

Tell a Friend!

You should have lots of great photos and videos to share by now. Ask your sous chef to post your favorite food photos on Pinterest and Instagram, or share a video of your learning-to-cook experience on YouTube.

LESSON 5

Spaghetti & Meatballs

SERVES: 4–6

COMPLETE THE LESSON: 40 min

READY TO SERVE: 40 min

A Meal Worth Singing About

Spaghetti and meatballs is such an all-time favorite there's actually a song about it. You know the one, "On top of spaghetti, all covered with cheese, I lost my poor meatball, when somebody sneezed." Well, song or no song, you're going to have fun with this recipe because making homemade meatballs is like playing with clay but you get to eat your creations afterwards!

Get Prepared!

Here's a little Sneak Peek of how this recipe is made.

Note to the Chef

Squish, squeeze, squash! This meal isn't only delicious to eat it's really fun to make. Think about it—when do you ever get to play with your food (with both hands no less!) without getting in trouble for it? There's a lot to learn in this very "hands-on" lesson so get those hands washed and let's roll!

1 **Make** the meatballs.

2 **Make** the marinara sauce.

STACK UP YOUR KNOWLEDGE

Here's what you'll learn in this lesson.

SKILLS

- ☐ peel and mince garlic
- ☐ core tomatoes
- ☐ shape meatballs

TERMS

- ☐ mince
- ☐ dice

A

3 **Cook** the spaghetti.

4 **Plate it up and enjoy!**

Note to the Sous Chef

There's a lot of slicing, dicing, and chopping in this recipe so your role as sous chef is primarily to provide guidance as your young chef develops his or her knife skills and also to reinforce the importance of washing hands after handling raw meat. Other than that this is a pretty foolproof recipe so you can just sit back, relax, and enjoy the show!

COOKING KNOW-HOW

- ☐ tomato-based sauces
- ☐ kitchen safety *(handling raw meat)*
- ☐ timing it right
- ☐ cooking garlic

Get Prepared!

When you're ready to start cooking, watch *Recipe 5: Spaghetti & Meatballs.*

What You'll Need

. . . to make Spaghetti & Meatballs

Shopping List

- ground beef (1 lb)
- ground pork (1/2 lb)
- breadcrumbs (1/2 cup)
- Parmesan cheese (1/2 cup)
- egg (1)
- basil (dried)
- milk (1/2 cup)
- spaghetti noodles (1 lb)
- tomatoes (6 to 8 medium or 3 lb)
- onion (1 medium)
- garlic (2 or more cloves)
- sugar
- balsamic vinegar (optional)
- tomato paste (optional)

An Easy-Fix Option for this recipe can be downloaded for free at

www.yourkidscooking.net

Substitute two 15-oz cans of diced tomatoes to shorten the Get Set! time.

. . . and to

Complete Your Meal

garlic bread (oven-ready in a bag)
green salad (complete salad in a bag)

This meal provides protein, grains, and vegetables. But a fresh green salad goes great with spaghetti and it provides another excellent source of fresh, healthy vegetables.

Shopping Tip

The type of tomato you use isn't as important as whether or not they are ripe. Choose tomatoes that are deep red in color, firm to the touch, and feel heavy for their size. Give them the smell test too—ripe tomatoes should smell like tomatoes!

What's On Your Plate?

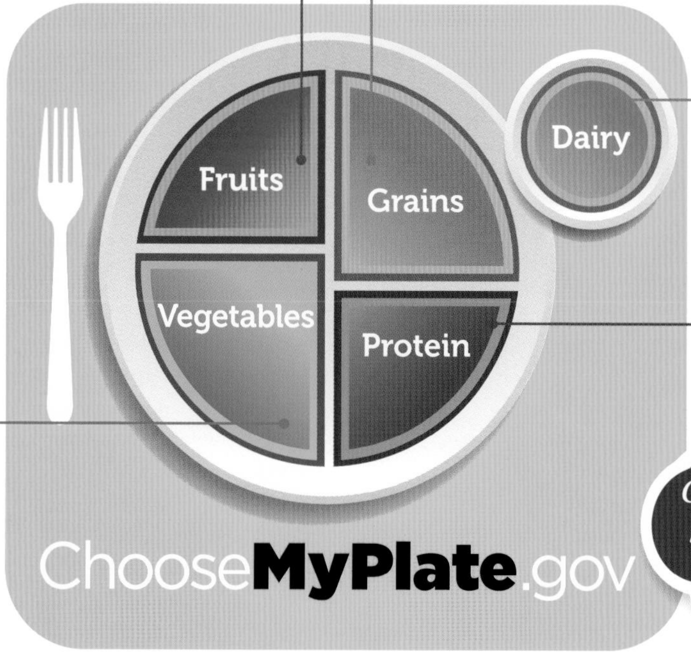

Fruits: none

Grains: pasta

Dairy: none

Protein: beef, pork

Vegetables: tomatoes, onions, lettuce

Empty Calories: ground beef, ground pork

Choose extra lean beef and pork to reduce the amount of empty calories from these foods.

In the Spotlight

Pasta is typically made with refined white flour, which is stripped of much of its nutrition during the refinement process. Whole-wheat pasta is a healthy and tasty alternative for this recipe.

Olive oil is high in fat, but 85% is monounsaturated fat, which is essential to a healthy diet.

Lettuce can be rich in vitamin K, which helps build strong bones. As a general rule, the darker green the leaves are, the more vitamins and minerals they contain. Iceberg lettuce has little nutritional value.

Why Whole Grains?

Eating whole grains, such as whole-wheat pasta, provides many health benefits and reduces the risk of some chronic diseases. Whole grains also contain a lot of fiber, making them a good fat-burning food. If you use whole-wheat pasta in dishes like spaghetti and meatballs, which are served with a rich and flavorful tomato-based sauce, you may not even taste the difference!

Get Ready!

Start *Recipe 5: Spaghetti & Meatballs* before completing this step.

Ingredients

ground beef

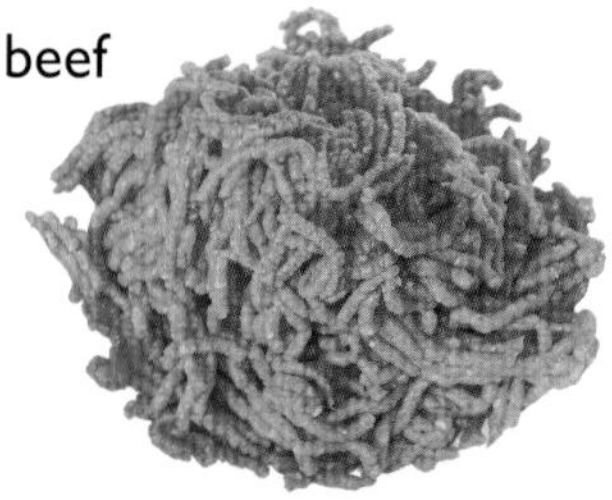

ground pork

breadcrumbs

Parmesan cheese

egg
(1)

basil *(dried)*

milk

spaghetti noodles
(1 lb)

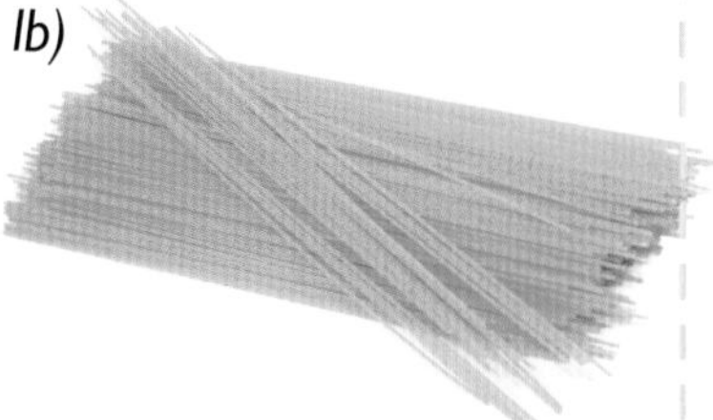

tomatoes *(6 to 8)*

onion
(1)

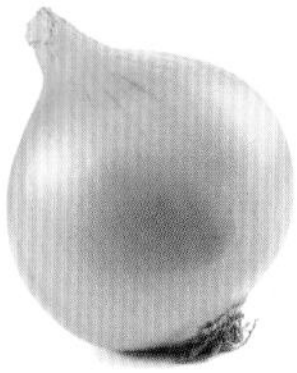

garlic
(2 or more cloves)

sugar

balsamic vinegar
(optional)

tomato paste
(optional)

Complete Your Meal

garlic bread (oven-ready in a bag)
green salad (complete salad in a bag)

No, this is not a candy store! It's a pasta shop in Venice, Italy. Bet you never saw striped pasta shaped like party hats in your grocery store!

Utensils

Cookware

baking tray *(large)*

stockpot

sauté pan *(large)*

Measurement

measuring cups

measuring spoons

Tools

paring knife

chef's knife

wooden spoon

tongs

bench scraper

tomato corer *(optional)*

Other

bowls *(2 small, 1 medium, 1 large)*

colander

cutting board(s)

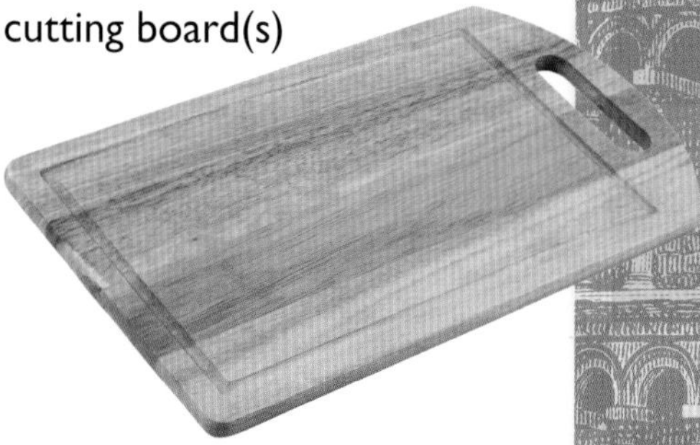

catch-all

Click CONTINUE when you're done!

Get Set!

Watch the *Get Set!* segment before completing these steps.

1 Make the meatballs.

- in large bowl, combine these ingredients:
  - **1 lb ground beef**
  - **½ lb ground pork**
  - **½ cup dried breadcrumbs**
  - **½ cup grated Parmesan cheese**
  - **1 egg**
  - **2 tsp basil**
  - **1 Tbsp salt**
  - **½ cup milk**
- form into golf golf ball-size meatballs (should yield about 36)
- arrange evenly on baking sheet
- wash your hands

Wet your hands before rolling the meatballs to keep the meat from sticking to them.

Be sure to make all the meatballs the same size so they cook evenly.

2 Dice the tomatoes.

- core and dice tomatoes; transfer to medium bowl

Make sure you take pictures as you go through the steps!

- chop onion into $\frac{1}{4}$-inch pieces; transfer to small bowl

3 Chop the onion.

- cut root end off 2–5 garlic cloves
- smash cloves under a flat surface to remove peel
- mince into tiny pieces; transfer to another small bowl

4 Peel and mince the garlic.

- fill stockpot $\frac{2}{3}$ full of water
- add some salt, cover, and heat on high setting
- preheat oven to 325°F

5 Preheat stuff.

Click CONTINUE when you're done!

Get Cooking!

Watch the *Get Cooking!* segment before completing these steps.

- bake meatballs uncovered at 325°F
- set a timer for 15 minutes

1 Bake the meatballs.

- cook onions in **1 Tbsp** olive oil for 3–4 minutes
- add garlic and cook another minute or less
- add tomatoes and:
  - **2 tsp salt**
  - **2–3 tsp basil**
  - **1 tsp sugar**
- simmer uncovered 15–20 minutes, stirring occasionally

2 Make the marinara sauce.

If your sauce isn't as thick as you'd like, add 1–2 Tbsp tomato paste.

- cook spaghetti according to directions on package

3 Cook the pasta.

4 Finish the marinara sauce.

- when meatballs are completely cooked, add to marinara sauce
- turn off burner; cover pan to keep meatballs warm

5 Drain the pasta.

- drain spaghetti; return to stockpot
- drizzle a little olive oil onto pasta to keep it from sticking together

Complete Your Meal

Ask your sous chef to prepare the green salad while the pasta cooks. Heat the garlic bread after the meatballs are done.

6 Plate it up and enjoy!

- top a serving of spaghetti with meatballs and sauce
- garnish with grated Parmesan cheese
- serve with garlic bread and fresh green salad

Happy Eating!

Test Your Skills!

Practice your new skills by making this tasty crowd-pleaser!

SERVES:
6–8

KITCHEN TIME:
30 min

READY TO SERVE:
1 hr 50 min

Meatloaf with Au Gratin Potatoes

Get Ready!

Ingredients

ground beef *(1 ½ lb)*

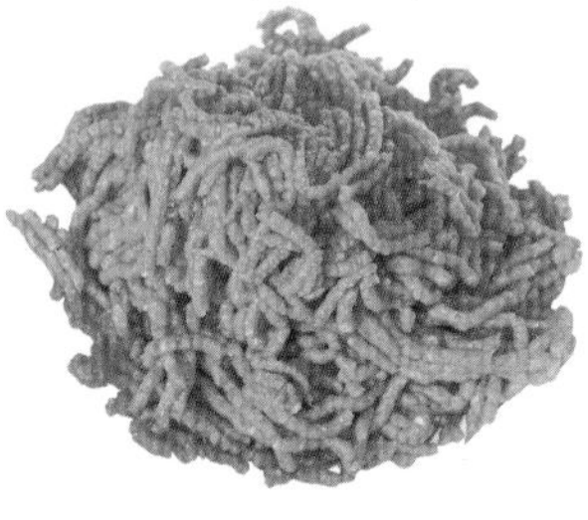

ground pork *(¾ lb)*

breadcrumbs *(½ cup dried)*

eggs *(2 large)*

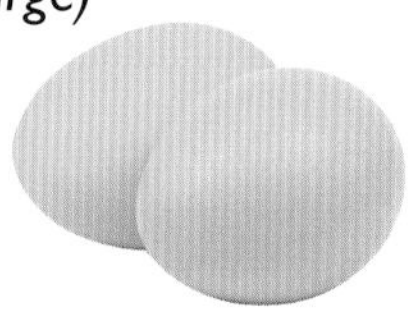

Italian seasoning

Worcestershire sauce

ketchup

russet potatoes *(6 large)*

onion
(1 medium)

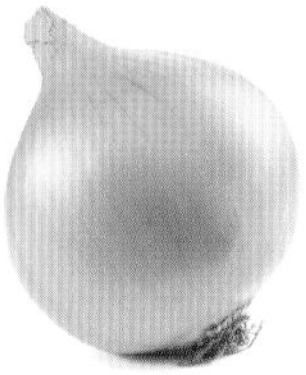

milk *(2 cups)*

cheddar cheese
(1 ½ cups grated)

flour

butter

oregano

OPTIONAL
green salad or vegetable

Utensils

COOKWARE
loaf pan *(9 x 5 in)*
casserole dish *(9 x 13 in)*
saucepan *(medium)*

TOOLS
chef's knife
whisk
bench scraper

MEASUREMENT
measuring cups
measuring spoons
liquid measuring cup

OTHER
bowls *(2 large)*
cutting board(s)
catch-all

Spaghetti & Meatballs

Preheat the oven to 350°F before you start the *Get Set!* steps.

STACK UP YOUR KNOWLEDGE

Don't forget to check off the STACK items you mastered on page 142.

Get Set!

350° Pre-heat

1 Make the meatloaf.

- in large bowl, combine:
  - 1 ½ lb ground beef
  - ¾ lb ground pork
  - ½ cup dried breadcrumbs
  - 2 eggs
  - 2 tsp Italian seasoning
  - 2 tsp Worcestershire sauce
  - ⅓ cup ketchup
  - 2 tsp salt
  - 1 tsp pepper
- place mixture into loaf pan

2 Slice the onion.

- slice onion into ¼-inch slices; transfer to large bowl

3 Grate the cheese.

- grate 1 ½ cups cheddar cheese

4 Measure ingredients for the Mornay sauce.

- 2 cups milk
- 3 Tbsp butter
- 3 Tbsp flour

5 Slice the potatoes.

- slice potatoes into ⅛-inch slices
- toss together with onions

Get Cooking!

1 Make the Mornay sauce.

- make a roux using flour and butter *(See page 24 to review how to make a roux.)*
- add milk, ½ tsp salt, and 2 tsp oregano
- turn off burner; add cheese; stir until melted

2 Assemble and bake the potatoes.

- arrange potatoes and onions in greased casserole dish; season with salt and pepper
- pour Mornay sauce over potatoes
- bake potatoes for about 1 ½ hours at 350°F or until potatoes are fork tender and top is golden brown

3 Bake the meatloaf.

- bake meatloaf uncovered about 1 hour at 350°F

4 Plate it up and enjoy!

- plate up with a fresh vegetable and enjoy!

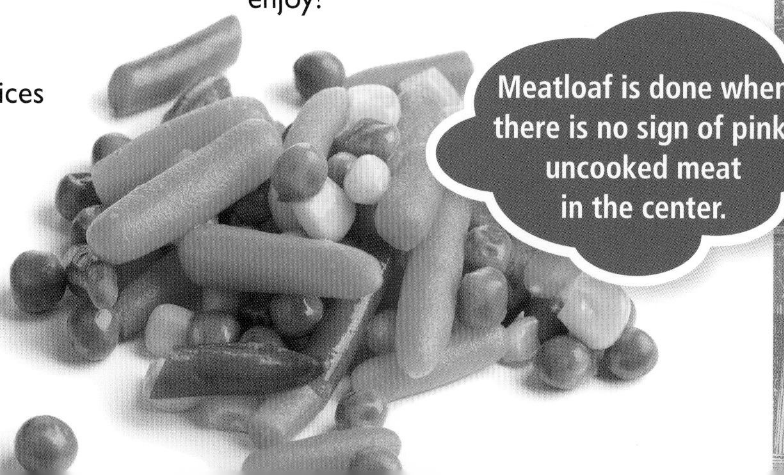

Meatloaf is done when there is no sign of pink, uncooked meat in the center.

Oatmeal Fruit Bars

Oatmeal bars are a great anytime snack. The oats provide whole-grain goodness and you get some fruit in your diet too! Make this recipe once, then get creative and try adding bran, nuts, or seeds. Anything goes with oatmeal bars!

What You'll Need

- 1 ½ sticks butter, cut up
- 2 tsp softened butter (to grease pan)
- 1 cup dried fruit (raisins, cranberries, apricots, etc.)
- 1 ½ cups rolled oats
- 1 cup all-purpose flour
- 1 cup firmly-packed brown sugar
- ¼ tsp salt
- ½ tsp cinnamon
- 1 tsp vanilla extract

Chop larger fruit, such as apricots, into small pieces.

What You'll Do

1. Melt the butter in microwave or small pot.
2. Preheat the oven to 350°F.
3. Grease a 9-inch-square baking pan.
4. In a medium bowl, mix together thoroughly: oats, flour, brown sugar, salt, cinnamon.
5. Add fruit, melted butter, and vanilla to the bowl; stir until well blended.
6. Press the dough into the pan until flat.
7. Bake 35–40 minutes or until golden brown.
8. Cool on a rack; cut into 12 bars.

Expand Your Horizons!

Practice everything you've learned so far making any of these recipes!

Swedish Meatballs
Stuffed Meatloaf
Meatball Soup
Creamy Sausage Pasta
Turkey Meatloaf
Salmon Burgers
Spinach Balls
Clam Linguini
Crab Cakes
Crunchy Ice Cream Balls

The recipes above, and many more, are available for download at

www.yourkidscooking.net

Tell a Friend!

Do you have any friends that would like to learn to cook? Invite them over when you make the next recipe and let them share in the fun. It's always more fun to cook with a friend!

LESSON 6

Stir-Fry

SERVES: 4

COMPLETE THE LESSON: 35 min

READY TO SERVE: 35 min

Moo Goo Gai What?

What do moo goo gai pan, chow fun, mapo doufu, and ants climbing a tree all have in common? Believe it or not, each one is a type of Asian stir-fry. To make a stir-fry you cook meat and vegetables very quickly over very high heat. Stir-frying is fast, healthy, and delicious—three excellent reasons to master this method and make it a regular part of your cooking repertoire.

Get Prepared!

Here's a little Sneak Peek of how this recipe is made.

Note to the Chef

This recipe is really going to put your knife skills to the test! You're going to chop, slice, dice, and mince your way to learning one of the most versatile and useful cooking methods there is. Stir-fry is a method of cooking where you fry bite-size pieces of your favorite meat (or poultry, fish or seafood, for that matter) and vegetables in a small amount of oil over high heat very quickly. It's fast and flavorful and a whole lot of fun, so get out those knives and let's get started! Chop-chop!

1 **Cut up** vegetables and chicken.

2 **Stir-fry** the chicken and vegetables.

STACK UP YOUR KNOWLEDGE

Here's what you'll learn in this lesson.

SKILLS

- □ peel vegetables
- □ slice celery
- □ prepare peapods
- □ slice peppers

TERMS

- □ vegetable peeler
- □ slurry
- □ stir-fry
- □ wok

A

3 **Cook** the rice.

4 **Plate it up and enjoy!**

Note to the Sous Chef

Although learning the stir-fry method of cooking is pretty easy, the key to success is in the preparation of the ingredients. Since most of the ingredients need to be cut up in one way or another, there is a lot of knife work involved. Sous chef supervision is recommended throughout the entire process, not only to keep things safe, but also to ensure that the ingredients are cut into uniform pieces of the right size. Also, due to different cooking times, it's important that the ingredients are added to the wok in the proper order and at the right time. When stir-frying, more so than with any other cooking method, timing is everything!

COOKING KNOW-HOW

- ☐ cooking with oil
- ☐ boiling rice
- ☐ best oils for stir-frying
- ☐ stir-frying basics
- ☐ Chinese spices

Get Prepared!

When you're ready to start cooking, watch *Recipe 6: Stir-Fry.*

What You'll Need

. . . to make Stir-Fry

Shopping List

- chicken breasts (2 boneless, skinless)
- rice (1 cup)
- water chestnuts (1 8-oz can, sliced)
- bamboo shoots (1 8-oz can)
- carrots (2 large)
- celery (2 stalks)
- red pepper (1 large)
- snow peas (8 oz)
- cornstarch
- soy sauce
- stir-fry oil
- Chinese five-spice powder
- chicken broth (1 15-oz can)
- crunchy chow mein noodles (1 5-oz can)

An Easy-Fix Option for this recipe can be downloaded for free at

www.yourkidscooking.net

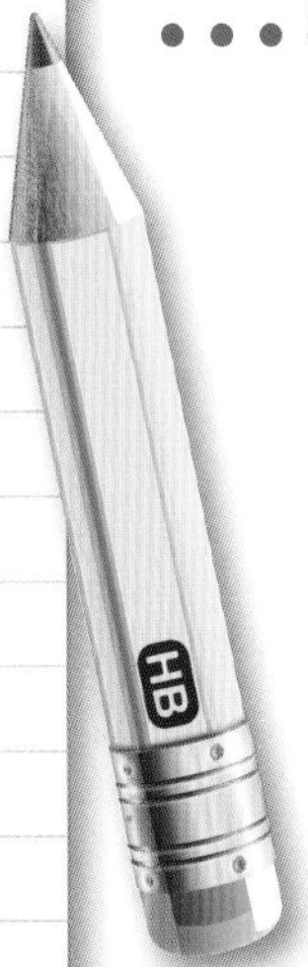

Because you'll be cooking at very high heat, you'll want to use a high smoking-point oil like peanut, safflower, corn, or canola. Peanut oil is a popular choice for stir-frying because it adds a pleasant nutty flavor.

. . . and to Complete Your Meal

There's no need for side dishes. This stir-fry is a complete and balanced meal all by itself! Serve on brown rice to get those whole-grains in your daily diet.

Shopping Tip

When buying chicken, look for secure, unbroken packaging and check the "sell-by" date. Inspect the chicken carefully. Its skin should be creamy white to deep yellow, not gray or pasty. If you notice a strong, unpleasant odor after opening the package, do not use the chicken. Return it promptly in its original package to the store for a refund.

What's On Your Plate?

Try brown rice to get those healthy whole grains you need!

none | rice

Empty Calories
none

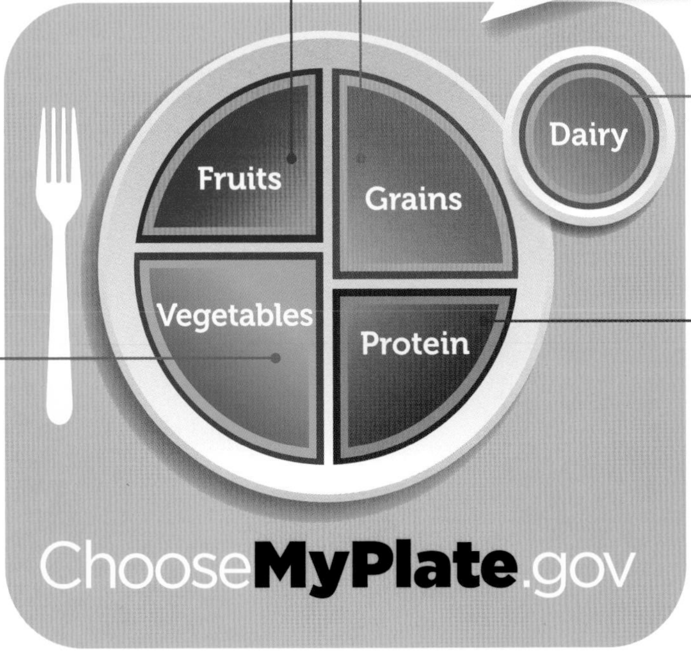

none

chicken breast

carrots
celery
peppers
snow peas
water chestnuts
bamboo shoots

There is no dairy in this meal. Serve low- or non-fat yogurt with fruit and granola for a light and healthy after-meal treat!

In the Spotlight

Chicken breast, without the skin, is an excellent source of lean protein. A chicken breast with the skin on has almost twice the calories and fat as skinless chicken breast, adding a lot of empty calories to an otherwise lean source of protein.

Stir-frying is a very healthy and low-fat way to prepare foods because foods are cooked quickly with little oil. Cooking vegetables quickly over high heat also helps to preserve their vitamins and minerals, especially in green vegetables.

Rice is an excellent source of energy. Brown rice—a whole grain—is healthier than white rice because it contains fiber and higher amounts of vitamins and minerals.

Oil and Empty Calories

Oils are fats that are liquid at room temperature like the vegetable oils used in cooking. Vegetable oils provide essential nutrients and are not considered empty calories. These oils are high in "good" fats, low in "bad" fats, and do not contain any cholesterol. A few plant oils, however, including coconut oil, palm oil, and palm kernel oil, are high in saturated fats. These oils, along with butter and shortening, are considered solid fats and contain empty calories.

Get Ready!

Start *Recipe 6: Stir-Fry* before completing this step.

Ingredients

chicken breasts* *(2)*

rice

water chestnuts *(1 8-oz can)*

bamboo shoots *(1 8-oz can)*

carrots *(2)*

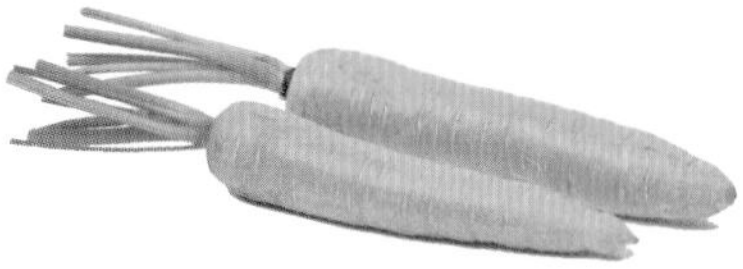

celery *(2 stalks)*

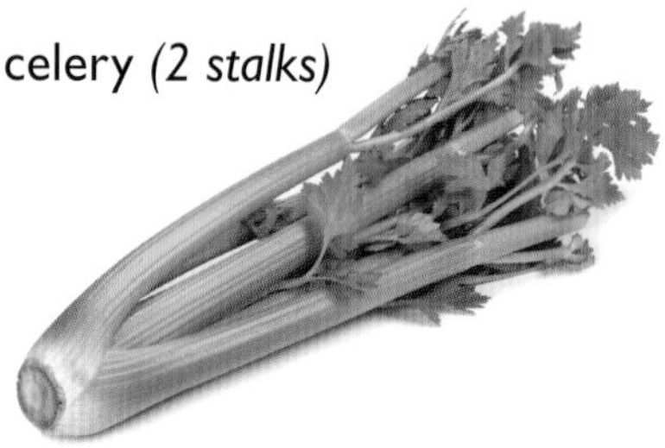

red pepper *(1)*

crunchy chow mein noodles

snow peas *(8 oz)*

cornstarch

soy sauce

stir-fry oil

Chinese five-spice powder

chicken broth *(1 15-oz can)*

Chinese cooking techniques vary widely in form, with stir-frying being one of the better-known methods in the West. But don't try the "flaming wok" trick at home—leave that for the professionals!

*Wrap chicken breasts in plastic wrap and place in the freezer for 15–20 minutes to make it easier to cut up.

Utensils

Cookware

saucepan *(medium)*

wok

Measurement

liquid measuring cup *(1 cup)*

measuring cups

measuring spoons

Tools

vegetable peeler

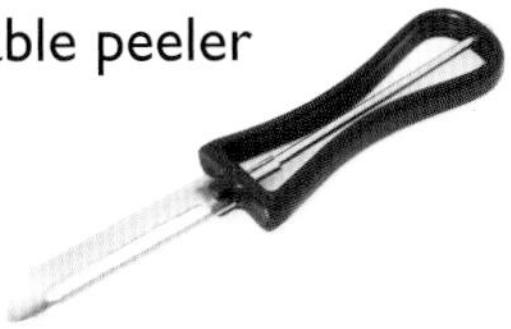

chef's knife

wooden spoon

flat spatula

can opener

whisk

Other

bowls *(1 small, 5 medium)*

colander

plastic wrap

cutting boards(s)

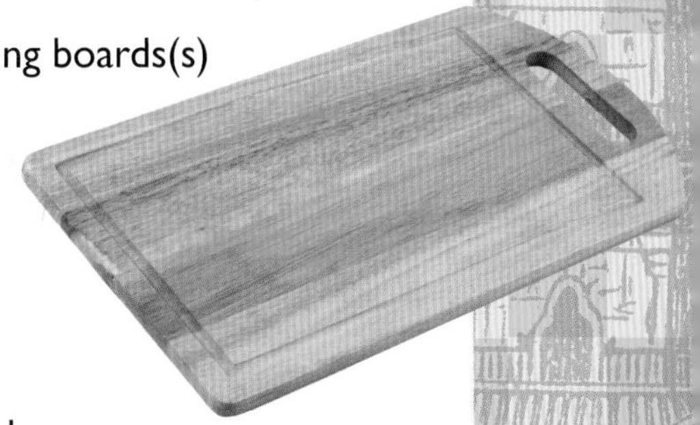

bench scraper

catch-all

Click CONTINUE when you're done!

Watch the *Get Set!* segment before completing these steps.

- measure **1 cup rice**
- measure **2 cups water** into saucepan
- add **1 tsp salt**, cover, and bring to boil over medium high heat

1 Prepare to cook the rice.

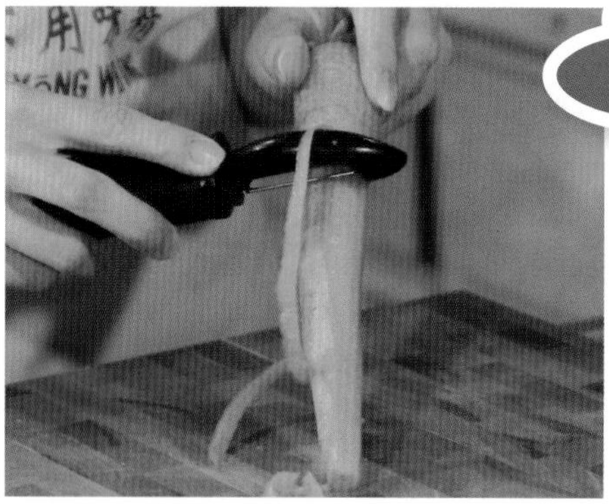

A 1/8-inch slice is about as wide as a nickel.

- peel carrots
- cut into 1/8-inch slices
- transfer to small bowl

2 Peel and slice the carrots.

3 Slice the celery.

- wash celery
- cut into 1/8-inch slices
- transfer to medium bowl

- cut off the stem end
- cut the pepper in half from top to bottom
- remove the pith and seeds
- slice pepper into ½-inch slices
- add to the bowl with the celery

4 Slice the red pepper.

- snap off stem end
- gently pull off the string that runs down the spine
- snap off flower end as needed

5 Prepare the pea pods.

- open and drain the water chestnuts and bamboo shoots in colander
- open canned chicken broth

6 Open the canned items.

- in a liquid measuring cup, combine:
  - **1 Tbsp cornstarch**
  - **2 Tbsp water**
  - **¼ cup soy sauce**
  - **2–3 tsp Chinese five-spice powder**
  - **1 can chicken broth**

7 Make the stir-fry sauce.

Make sure all the pieces are the same size to ensure even cooking.

- cut chicken breasts into bite-size pieces
- transfer to medium bowl
- wash your hands and all the utensils that touched the raw chicken

8 Dice up the chicken.

Click CONTINUE when you're done!

Get Cooking!

Watch the *Get Cooking!* segment before completing these steps.

- add rice to the boiling water
- stir to loosen rice
- adjust heat to maintain a slow simmer
- cover and cook according to the directions on the package

1 Cook the rice.

- heat **1–2 Tbsp oil** in wok
- add chicken to hot wok
- cook chicken 2–4 minutes, stirring constantly
- check to make sure chicken pieces are cooked through
- transfer to a clean bowl

2 Stir-fry the chicken.

- add more oil to wok if needed
- add carrots; stir-fry 1–2 minutes
- add celery and peppers; stir-fry until they start to soften
- add water chestnuts and bamboo shoots; stir-fry until they are just heated through
- add pea pods; stir-fry until they begin to soften slightly

3 Stir-fry the vegetables.

Make sure you take pictures as you go through the steps!

- return the cooked chicken to the wok
- pour in sauce; stir until it thickens
- turn off burner; remove wok from heat

4 **Finish** the stir-fry.

- serve stir-fry over rice
- top with crunchy noodles

5 **Plate it up and enjoy!**

Happy Eating!

Test Your Skills!

Here's another classic stir-fry you can make to practice your new skills.

SERVES:
4

KITCHEN TIME:
30 min

READY TO SERVE:
30 min

Cashew Chicken

Get Ready!

Ingredients

chicken breast *(2 boneless, skinless)*

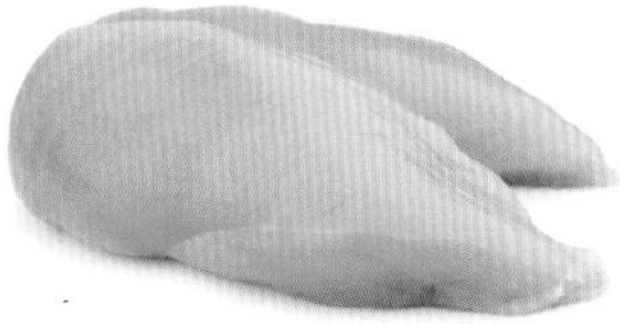

celery *(4 stalks)*

water chestnuts *(1 8-oz can, sliced)*

soy sauce

chicken broth *(1 15-oz can)*

cornstarch

rice vinegar

hoisin sauce

ginger *(ground)*

Chinese five-spice

sugar *(optional)*

stir-fry oil

sesame oil

cashews *(½ cup roasted, unsalted)*

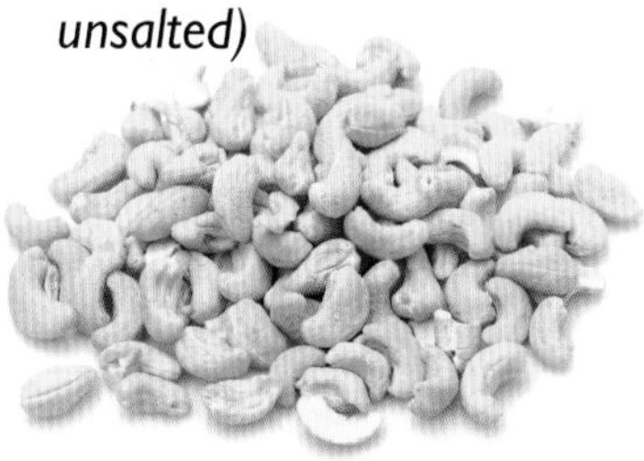

rice

Utensils

COOKWARE

wok *(or large frying pan)*
saucepan *(medium)*

TOOLS

chef's knife
can opener
flat spatula
whisk

MEASUREMENT

liquid measuring cup
measuring spoons

OTHER

bowls *(1 medium)*
colander
resealable plastic bag
cutting board(s)
bench scraper
catch-all

Stir-Fry

STACK UP YOUR KNOWLEDGE

Don't forget to check off the STACK items you mastered on page 142.

Get Set!

1 Marinade the chicken.

- cut chicken breasts into bite-size pieces
- in the plastic bag, combine:
  - 2 Tbsp soy sauce
  - 1 tsp Chinese five-spice
  - 1 tsp sesame oil
- add chicken, seal bag, and turn to coat
- refrigerate for up to 30 minutes

2 Make the stir-fry sauce.

- in a liquid measuring cup, whisk together:
  - 1 can chicken broth
  - 2 Tbsp cornstarch
  - 1 Tbsp rice vinegar
  - 2 Tbsp hoisin sauce
  - ½ tsp ginger
  - 1 Tbsp soy sauce
  - ½ tsp sugar (optional)

3 Prepare the veggies.

- cut celery into ¼-inch pieces
- open and drain water chestnuts

4 Prepare the rice.

- into the medium saucepan, add:
  - 2 cups water
  - 1 tsp salt
- cover and heat over high heat
- measure 1 cup rice

Get Cooking!

1 Cook the rice.

- add rice to boiling water
- reduce heat to maintain a simmer
- cover and cook about 20 minutes, or until liquid is absorbed

2 Stir-fry the chicken.

- heat 1 Tbsp stir-fry oil in wok over high heat
- add chicken
- stir-fry until no longer pink inside, adjusting heat as necessary to keep from burning
- remove to a paper towel

3 Stir-fry the veggies.

- heat more oil in wok if necessary
- add celery, onions and water chestnuts
- stir-fry over high heat until celery is just tender, adjusting heat as necessary to keep from burning

4 Finish the stir-fry.

- return chicken to the pan
- add sauce; continue to cook until sauce thickens
- add cashews

5 Plate it up and enjoy!

- serve stir-fry over rice
- garnish with additional cashews

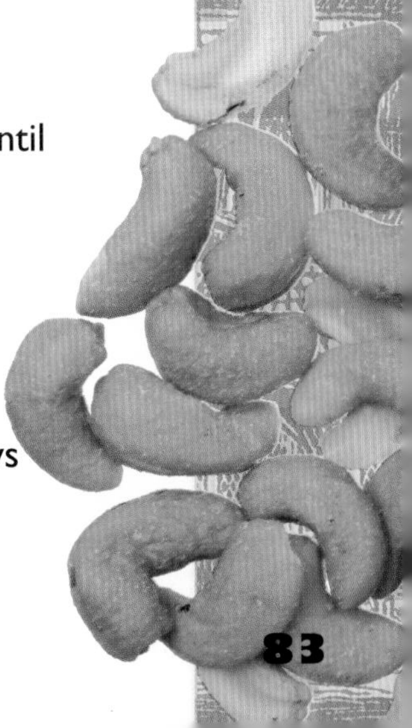

Reward Yourself!

Easy Key Lime Pie

For more than 100 years Southerners have been enjoying sweet-and-tart Key Lime Pie—the official pie of Florida. "Baked" in the refrigerator, this cool and refreshing dessert really hits the spot on a hot summer day.

What You'll Need

- 1 9-in graham cracker pie crust
- 1 package (Key) Lime gelatin (small)
- 2 6-oz containers of Key Lime yogurt
- frozen whipped topping (8 oz)

What You'll Do

1. In a medium bowl, combine gelatin and ¼ cup boiling water.
2. Stir until gelatin is completely dissolved.
3. Add yogurt and whipped topping.
4. Stir until thoroughly combined.
5. Pour into graham cracker crust.
6. Refrigerate until set.

Expand Your Horizons!

Practice everything you've learned so far by making one or all of these delicious recipes.

Fajitas
Chow Mein
Broccoli Beef
Beef Noodle Bowl
Sausage-Stuffed Bell Peppers
Beef and Potato Pasties
Chicken Ragu
Pasta Primavera
Vegetable Fried Rice
Chicken Noodle Soup

The recipes above, and many more, are available for download at

www.yourkidscooking.net

Tell a Friend!

Share your favorite Reward Yourself! recipes and pictures with your friends and family. Invite your friends to try some of the recipes and tell you how they turned out. Ask them to share one of their favorite recipes too!

LESSON 7

Eggs Benedict

SERVES: 2–4

COMPLETE THE LESSON: 40 min

READY TO SERVE: 40 min

Its Own National Holiday?

Yes, April 16th is National Eggs Benedict Day! But isn't it funny that a dish that is so popular to eat is also a dish most people are afraid to make! Hollandaise sauce—the key ingredient—has a reputation for being really tricky to make. But that's only if you don't know what you're doing. Once you understand the basics you'll see it's actually really quick and simple to make, not to mention delicious!

Get Prepared!

Here's a little Sneak Peek of how this recipe is made.

Note to the Chef

It's time to warm up those biceps, chefs, because this recipe is a real muscle builder! Hollandaise sauce is actually quite quick and easy to prepare. It does, however, require a lot of fast and furious whisking of egg yolks and butter as they cook very slowly over very low heat. But while it may require a little more muscle power than most recipes, it's so worth it! So start flexing those muscles and together we'll "whisk" up a masterpiece!

1 **Cook** the Canadian bacon.

2 **Make** Hollandaise sauce from eggs and butter.

STACK UP YOUR KNOWLEDGE

Here's what you'll learn in this lesson.

SKILLS

- ☐ separate eggs
- ☐ poach eggs
- ☐ chop herbs

TERMS

- ☐ poach
- ☐ separate eggs
- ☐ double-boiler

A

3 **Poach** eggs in simmering water.

4 **Plate it up and enjoy!**

Note to the Sous Chef
Despite what you may have heard, Hollandaise sauce is not nearly as difficult to make as legend has it. As long as the chef can crack and whisk eggs, success is in the bag—or in this case, the pan! The worst that can happen is the sauce may separate. It will still taste great, it just won't have the creamy, silky texture that it should. Your young chefs are well prepared for this, so please, carry on with confidence!

COOKING KNOW-HOW

- ☐ using a double-boiler
- ☐ making Hollandaise sauce
- ☐ poaching eggs

Get Prepared!

When you're ready to start cooking, watch *Recipe 7: Eggs Benedict.*

What You'll Need

. . . to make Eggs Benedict

Shopping List

- eggs (8 large)
- Canadian bacon (4 slices)
- English muffins (2)
- potatoes (4)
- lemon (1)
- cooking oil
- butter (1 stick + 1 Tbsp)
- vinegar
- parsley (for garnish)
- cayenne pepper (optional)

An Easy-Fix Option for this recipe can be downloaded for free at

www.yourkidscooking.net

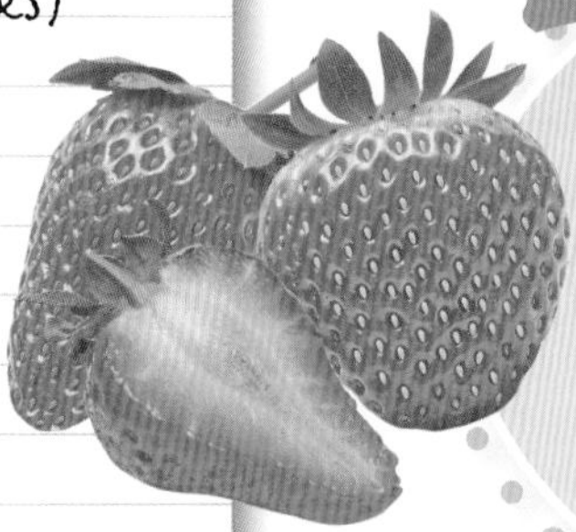

. . . and to Complete Your Meal

fresh fruit
(such as oranges, strawberries, and kiwi)

Eggs Benedict is packed with protein, but not much else. Serve with fresh fruit to make it a more nutritionally complete meal. Also, eggs Benedict is high in fat and empty calories, so keep portions small.

Shopping Tip

Canadian bacon is more like ham than bacon. If you can't find real "Canadian bacon" in your grocery store, you can substitute ham. If you use ham, be careful not to overcook it or it will get dry and tough.

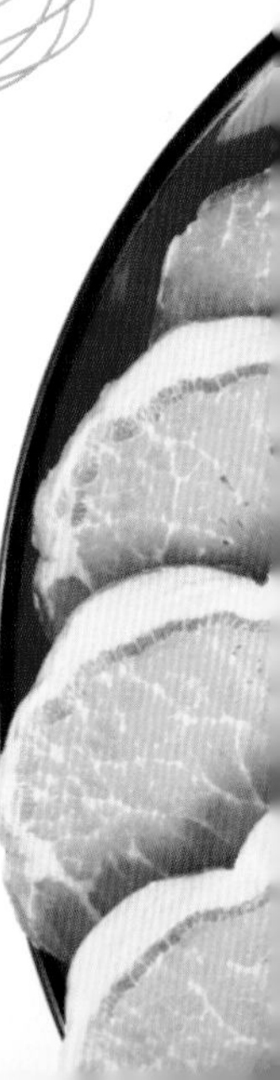

What's On Your Plate?

Try whole-wheat or whole-grain English muffins.

oranges, strawberries, kiwi

English muffins

Empty Calories
butter

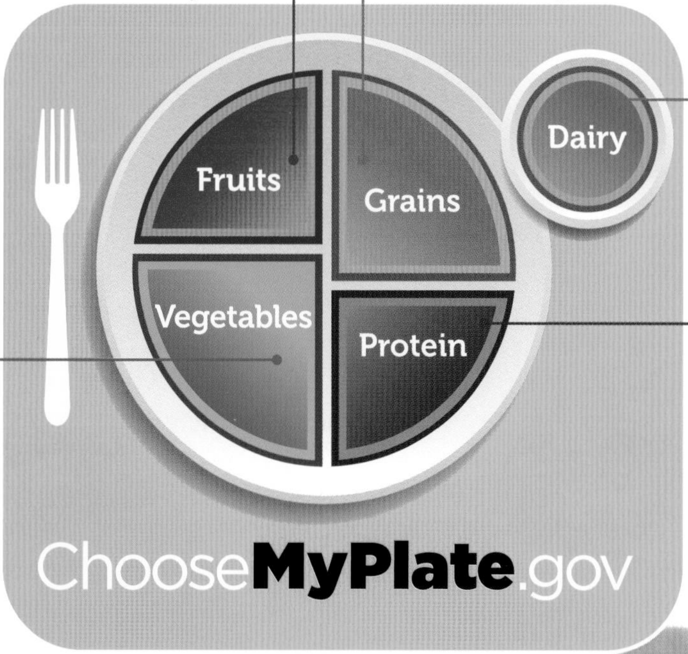

none

potatoes

eggs
Canadian bacon

IN THE Spotlight

Canadian bacon is a good source of protein and because it is made from the back of the pig, and not the belly like regular cured bacon, it contains about 1/3 less fat.

Butter is a solid fat, which means it is solid at room temperature. Solid fats come mainly from animal foods and are high in saturated fats and cholesterol. Like refined sugars, they are considered "empty calories" because they add calories and little, if any, nutrition. It is important to limit the number of empty calories you eat.

Eggs have the highest quality protein of any food and are full of all sorts of other essential nutrients. However, they are also high in fat so limit your consumption to 5–7 eggs a week.

Eat a Rainbow of Fruits and Veggies

Choose fruit in a variety of colors, like apples, strawberries, oranges, and bananas. Half your plate should be fruits and vegetables so add fruits and vegetables to your meals as side dishes or serve as dessert.

Get Ready!

Start *Recipe 7: Eggs Benedict* before completing this step.

Ingredients

eggs *(8)*

Canadian bacon *(4 slices)*

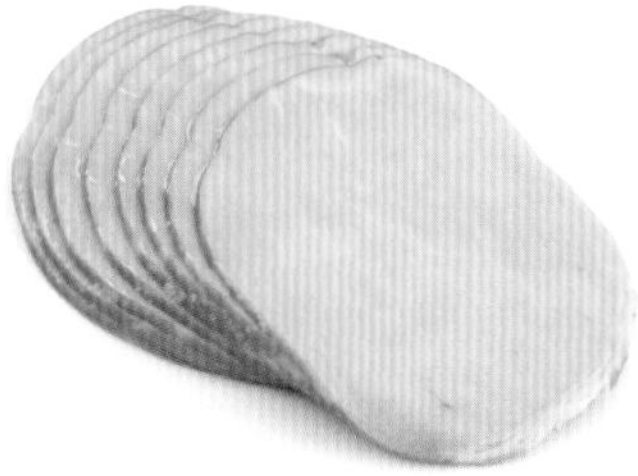

English muffins *(2)*

potatoes *(4)*

lemon *(1)*

cooking oil

butter *(1 stick)*

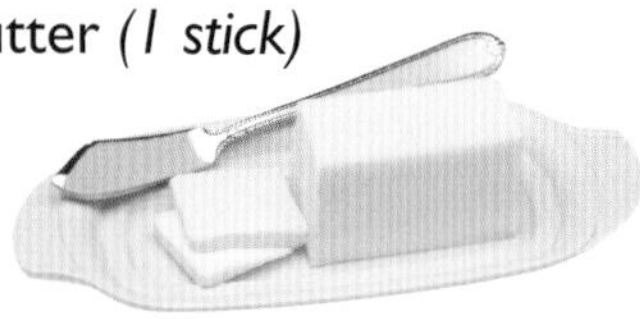

vinegar

parsley *(fresh)*

cayenne pepper *(optional)*

Guess What!

A kiwi fruit has up to five times more vitamin C than an orange and is also a good source of fiber. You can even eat the furry skin if you want to! Pineapples, strawberries and most other fruits are also good sources of vitamin C, which is excellent for your skin, hair, and nails and also helps to boost your immune system.

Complete Your Meal

fresh fruit

Legend has it that in 1894, Lemuel Benedict, a member of New York's high-society, ordered poached eggs, bacon, toast and Hollandaise sauce then built the dish that now bears his name. Over 100 years later Eggs Benedict is still one of the most popular breakfast items in America.

Utensils

Cookware

frying pan *(medium)*

double-boiler

If you don't have a double-boiler, place a glass or metal bowl in a saucepan. The bottom of the bowl should be about 2 inches above the bottom of the pan.

sauté pan *(medium)*

Measurement

measuring spoons

Tools

paring knife

chef's knife

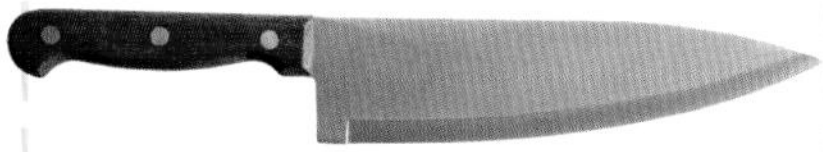

flat spatula

whisk

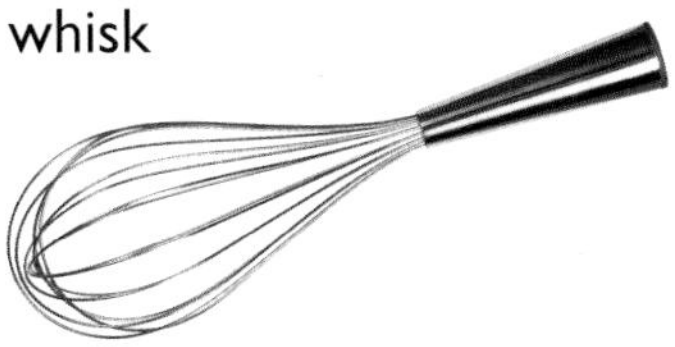

slotted spoon

Other

bowls *(4 small, 1 medium)*

catch-all

Click CONTINUE when you're done!

Get Set!

Watch the *Get Set!* segment before completing these steps.

- scrub potatoes under running water
- poke several times with fork
- cook in microwave until fork tender *(time varies)*

1 **Precook** the potatoes.

- measure and set aside **3 Tbsp butter**
- cut remaining butter into small chunks; transfer to small bowl

2 **Cut up** the butter.

3 **Prepare** the lemon for juicing.

- roll and squish lemon on hard surface to soften it
- cut 2 slits in tip with paring knife

- separate 4 egg yolks into a small bowl

4 **Separate** the eggs.

Make sure you take pictures as you go through the steps!

Make sure all the potato pieces are the same size so they cook evenly!

- cut cooked potatoes into small, bite-size pieces

5 **Cut up** the potatoes.

- finely chop **1–2 Tbsp parsley** using chef's knife

6 **Chop** the parsley.

Make sure the water in the pan does not touch the insert.

- add an inch or so of water to saucepan
- preheat water over medium-high heat

7 **Prepare** the double-boiler.

- add 1–2 inches of water to sauté pan
- add about **1 tsp vinegar**
- preheat water over medium heat

8 **Prepare** the poaching water.

Click CONTINUE when you're done!

Get Cooking!

Watch the *Get Cooking!* segment before completing these steps.

Complete Your Meal

Ask your sous chef to prepare the fresh fruit while you cook the bacon.

1 Cook the Canadian bacon.

- melt **1 Tbsp butter** in frying pan
- cook Canadian bacon over medium heat until browned
- remove to paper towel

2 Fry the potatoes.

- in frying pan, on medium-high, heat:
  - **1 Tbsp oil**
  - **1 Tbsp butter**
- add potatoes to hot pan; season with salt and pepper
- cook potatoes 7–10 minutes or until brown and crispy
- proceed to Step 3 while potatoes cook; remember to stir occasionally

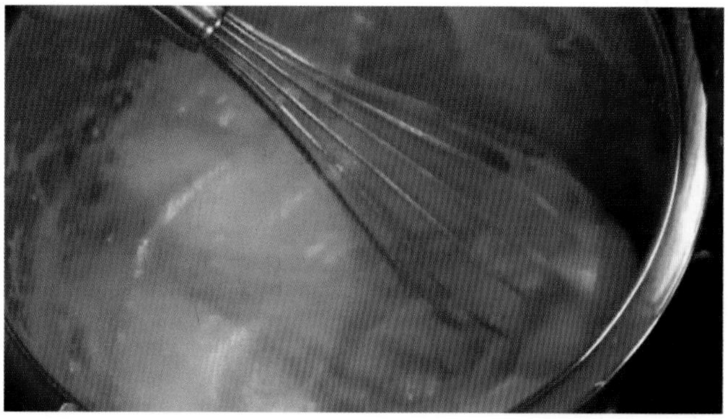

3 Make the Hollandaise sauce.

- adjust heat to maintain a simmer
- place insert in saucepan; add 1 Tbsp water
- add egg yolks; whisk until light yellow with foamy, airy texture
- add 2–3 pieces butter at a time, whisking continuously
- to the sauce, add:
  - **pinch of salt**
  - **squeeze of lemon juice**
  - **pinch of cayenne pepper**
- cook sauce until thickened ribbons drip off whisk
- turn off burner; remove pan from heat

Lift up the insert every minute or so to release the heat and keep it from getting too hot.

- toast and butter English muffins

4 **Toast** the English muffins.

- one at a time, crack the remaining 4 eggs into a small bowl then gently slide them into the poaching water
- let eggs cook, undisturbed, 4–5 minutes or until solid white
- remove eggs with slotted spoon; blot dry with paper towel

5 **Poach** the eggs.

- top each muffin with a slice of Canadian bacon, an egg, and Hollandaise sauce
- garnish with chopped parsley and a pinch of cayenne pepper

6 **Plate it up and enjoy!**

Happy Eating!

Test Your Skills!

Put your new skills to the test with this delicious and elegant classic.

SERVES:
4

KITCHEN TIME:
30 min

READY TO SERVE:
30 min

Poached Salmon with Béarnaise Sauce

Get Ready!

Ingredients

salmon fillets *(4 6-oz boneless, skinless)*

eggs *(4)*

butter *(1 stick)*

asparagus *(1 bunch)*

lemon *(1)*

tarragon *(1 Tbsp dried)*

olive oil

OPTIONAL
sliced fresh tomatoes
frozen steak fries

Utensils

COOKWARE
frying pans *(1 medium, 1 large)*
double boiler
sauté pan *(medium)*

TOOLS
paring knife
chef's knife
flat spatula
whisk
slotted spoon

MEASUREMENT
measuring spoons

OTHER
bowls *(4 small, 1 medium)*
catch-all

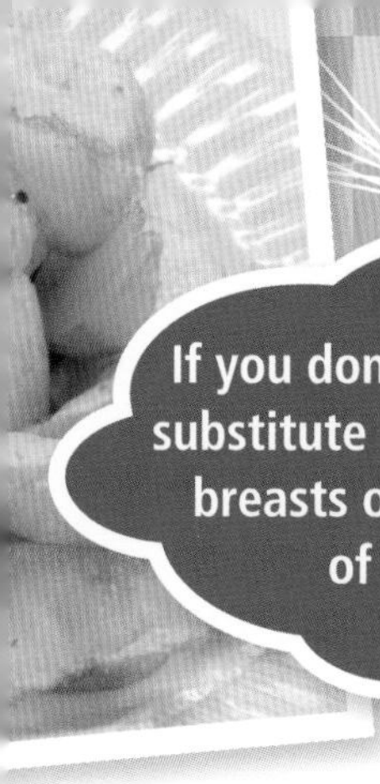

If you don't like salmon, substitute broiled chicken breasts or your choice of steaks.

STACK UP YOUR KNOWLEDGE

Don't forget to check off the STACK items you mastered on page 142.

Get Set!

1 Prepare the asparagus.

- wash and trim ends from asparagus
- place in frying pan; cover with water

2 Cut up the butter.

- cut 1 stick butter into small chunks
- set 1 Tbsp aside; place remaining pieces in small bowl

3 Prepare the lemon for juicing.

- roll and squish lemon on hard surface to soften
- cut 2 slits in tip with paring knife

4 Separate the eggs.

- crack and separate 4 egg yolks

5 Prepare the double-boiler.

- add an inch or so of water to saucepan; preheat over medium-high heat

6 Prepare the poaching water.

- to poaching pan, add:
  1 inch water
  1 Tbsp lemon juice
  1 Tbsp olive oil
  1 tsp salt, dash pepper
- add salmon and enough additional water to just cover salmon

Get Cooking!

1 Poach the salmon.

- heat salmon water until hot and steaming but not simmering
- poach salmon 5–10 minutes until it turns opaque and firm to touch
- pat dry with paper towel; cover with foil to keep warm

2 Boil the asparagus.

- bring asparagus water to simmer; cook to desired tenderness

3 Make the Bearnaise sauce.

- adjust heat to maintain simmer
- place insert in saucepan; add
  1 Tbsp water
- add egg yolks; whisk until light yellow and foamy
- add 2–3 pieces butter at a time, whisking continuously
- add a pinch of salt, a squeeze of lemon juice, and 1 Tbsp tarragon
- continue to cook sauce until it thickens up and forms ribbons as it drips off whisk
- turn off burner; remove pan from heat

4 Plate it up and enjoy!

- top salmon and asparagus with Béarnaise sauce

Chocolate Dipped Snacks

This recipe is so fun to make because you can experiment with turning all kinds of snacks into delicious chocolaty treats. Get creative and dip your favorite fruit, fresh or dried, graham crackers, pretzels, vanilla wafers... whatever your "inner-chef" desires!

Remember to wash the strawberries before dipping!

What You'll Need

- strawberries
- bananas
- graham crackers
- pretzels
- other favorite fruit or crackers
- semisweet chocolate chips *(6–8 oz)*

What You'll Do

1. Slice peeled bananas into bite-size pieces.
2. Set up a double boiler. *(See page 91 for instructions.)*
3. Melt the chocolate chips in the double boiler; stir often.
4. Turn heat to low to keep chocolate warm.
5. Dip the goodies into the chocolate to cover halfway; allow the excess chocolate to drip back into the bowl.
6. Place the dipper on a foil- or wax paper-lined baking tray.
7. Place the tray in the refrigerator until the chocolate has set.
8. Save any uneaten treats in an airtight container.

Expand Your Horizons!

Use everything you've learned so far to make all of these delicious recipes, and more!

Eggs Florentine
Arroz con Huevos
Corned Beef Hash with Poached Eggs
Steak Béarnaise
Herbed Chicken with Béarnaise Sauce
Huevos Rancheros (California Style)
Chicken Tortilla Soup
Sausage and Egg Breakfast Muffin
Rice Pudding
Chocolate Mousse

The recipes above, and many more, are available for download at

www.yourkidscooking.net

Tell a Friend!

Ask your sous chef to post reviews of the recipes you've made so far online and make recommendations for recipes your friends and family might want to try. Offer to help those who don't know how to cook yet. They will love you for it!

LESSON 8

Chicken Parmesan

SERVES: 4–6

COMPLETE THE LESSON: 40 min

READY TO SERVE: 1 hour 10 min

A Taste of Italy

Chicken Parmesan is a classic Italian dish that originated in the Parma region of Italy several centuries ago—thus the name chicken-PARME-san. Its signature ingredient is the famous cheese from the same region—Parmesan cheese. There's a reason this dish has become such a classic. Simply put—it's delicious!

Get Prepared!

Here's a little Sneak Peek of how this recipe is made.

Note to the Chef

It's time to warm up those muscles again because this is a great recipe to burn off a little extra energy. You're going to use a meat tenderizer (a "kitchen hammer", if you will) to flatten and tenderize chicken breasts. It's a lot of fun, but be careful to keep your fingers out of the way of the hammer! And of course, be sure to wash your hands after handling the raw chicken. A fun kitchen needs to be a safe and healthy kitchen, after all!

1 **Sauté** breaded chicken breasts.

2 **Cover** chicken with marinara sauce and cheese and bake.

STACK UP YOUR KNOWLEDGE

Here's what you'll learn in this lesson.

SKILLS

- ☐ pound chicken
- ☐ bread chicken
- ☐ slice cheese

TERMS

- ☐ breading
- ☐ sauté

A

3 **Cook** pasta and sauté vegetables.

4 **Plate it up and enjoy!**

Note to the Sous Chef
This recipe is really very basic and easy to prepare. The main skill taught is how to use a meat tenderizer to flatten and tenderize chicken breast. Using a meat tenderizer requires some muscle and a little technique, so your help with this part of the recipe may be needed. It's also important to make your chef aware of how to be safe from potentially harmful bacteria when handling raw chicken.

Cooking Know-How

- ☐ baking casseroles
- ☐ sautéing vegetables

Get Prepared!

When you're ready to start cooking, watch *Recipe 8: Chicken Parmesan.*

What You'll Need

... to make Chicken Parmesan

Shopping List

- chicken breasts (2 boneless, skinless)
- fettuccini (1 lb)
- breadcrumbs (1/4 cup)
- Parmesan cheese (1 cup)
- eggs (3)
- flour
- mozzarella cheese (3/4 pound)
- tomato (1)
- zucchini (2)
- yellow squash (2)
- garlic (1–2 cloves)
- onion (1)
- canned marinara sauce (24 oz)
- Italian seasoning
- oregano (dried)
- olive oil
- balsamic vinegar (optional)

An Easy-Fix Option for this recipe can be downloaded for free at www.yourkidscooking.net

... and to Complete Your Meal

garlic bread
(oven-ready in a bag)

Chicken Parmesan, when served with the sautéed vegetables, is a nutritionally complete meal. But crusty French bread compliments any pasta dish, so we recommend serving this meal with a loaf of oven-ready garlic bread.

Shopping Tip

Buying boneless, skinless chicken breasts in bulk can be a real time and money saver. Divide chicken into meal-size portions and package for freezing. In most recipes, one large breast is enough for 2 servings.

Food Storage Tip

Fresh, raw chicken can be stored in its original packaging for up to two days in the refrigerator. However, freeze chicken immediately if you do not plan to use it within two days after purchasing. You can safely freeze most chicken in its original packaging for up to two months.

What's On Your Plate?

none

fettuccini
breadcrumbs
garlic bread

Empty Calories
cheese

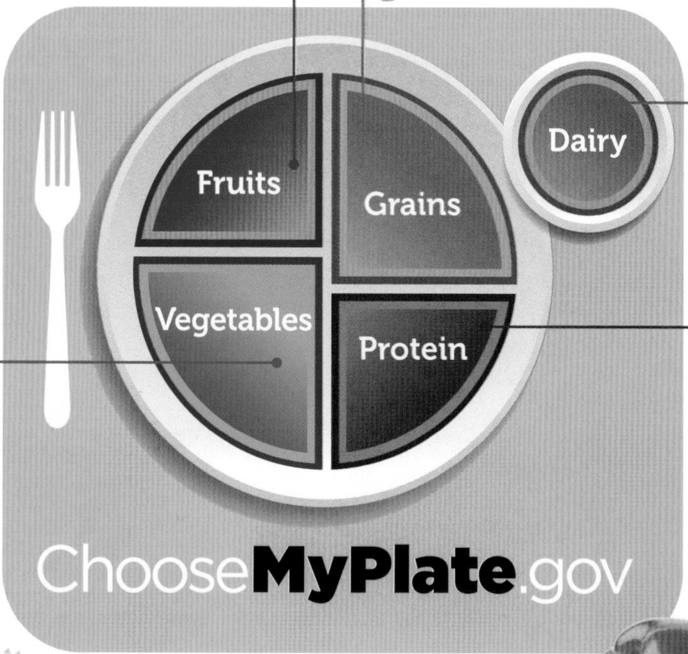

cheese

chicken
cheese

zucchini
yellow squash
tomatoes
onions

In the Spotlight

Tomatoes are a low-calorie vegetable with very low fat content and zero cholesterol. They are also an excellent source of antioxidants, dietary fiber, minerals, and vitamins. In fact, because of their all-round nutritional qualities, tomatoes have more health-benefiting properties than an apple!

Mozzarella cheese is a solid source of protein and can be a smarter choice than soft cheeses and rich hard cheeses, such as cheddar, because mozzarella tends to contain fewer calories and less saturated fat. There are two types of mozzarella cheese—whole-milk and part-skim. The main difference between the two is the amount of fat in each. Whole-milk mozzarella contains more fat and calories and less protein than part-skim mozzarella.

A Colorful Plate is a Healthy Plate!

Add color to your plate by choosing bright-colored vegetables, like red bell peppers, orange carrots, or green peas and broccoli. Different-colored vegetables contain different nutrients. Eating a variety of colors ensures you get a healthy mix of all the nutrients vegetables have to offer.

Start *Recipe 8: Chicken Parmesan* before completing this step.

Ingredients

chicken breasts *(2)*

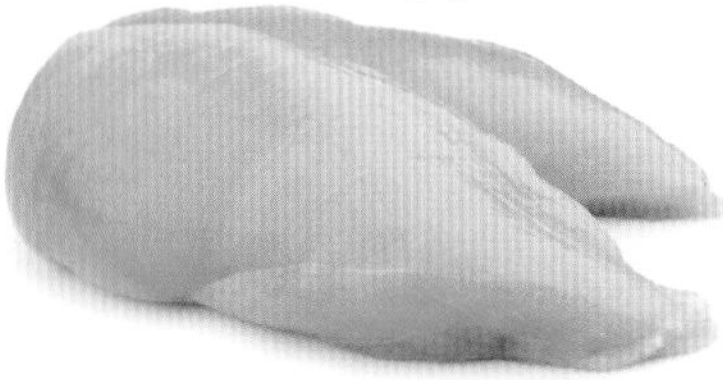

fettuccini *(1 lb)*

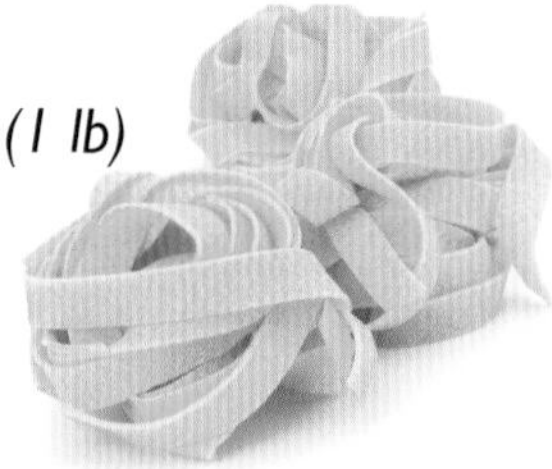

breadcrumbs

Parmesan cheese

eggs *(3 large)*

flour

mozzarella cheese

tomato *(1)*

zucchini *(2)*

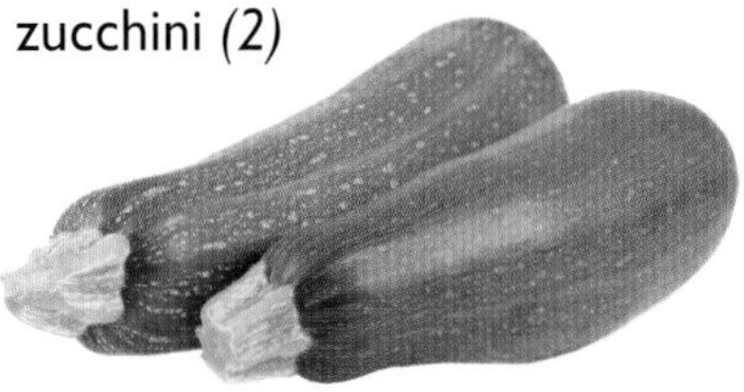

yellow squash *(2)*

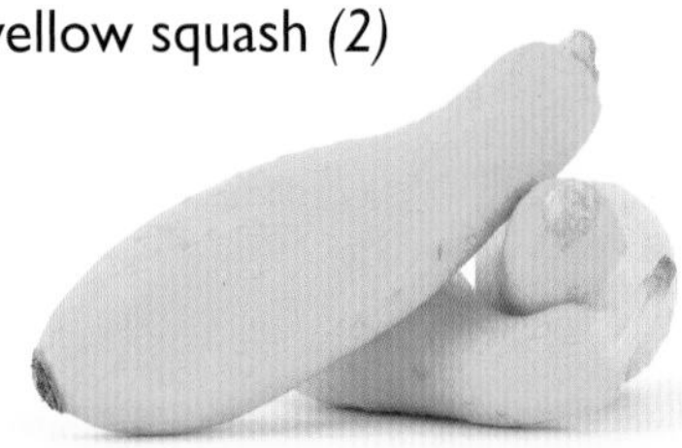

garlic *(1–2 cloves)*

onion *(1)*

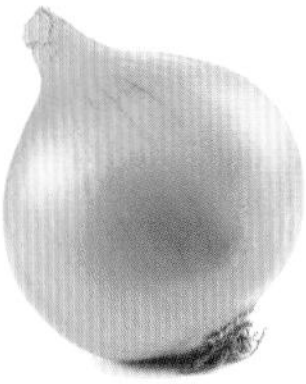

canned marinara sauce

Italian seasoning

oregano

olive oil

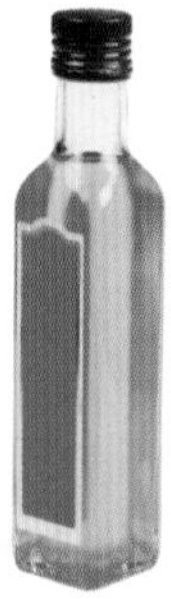

balsamic vinegar *(optional)*

Complete Your Meal

garlic bread
(oven-ready in a bag)

Utensils

Cookware

baking dish *(9 x 13 inches)*

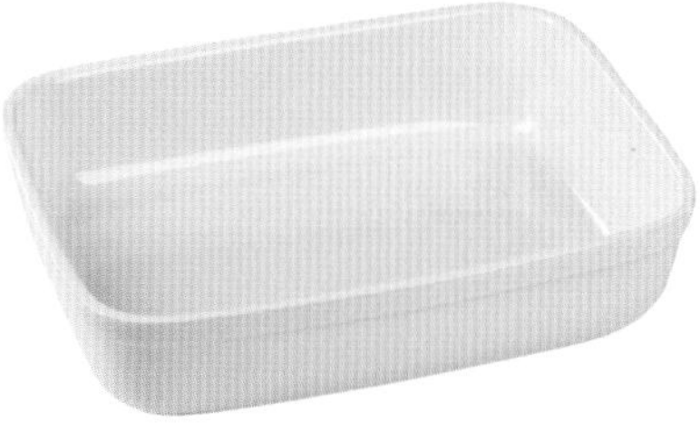

sauté pan *(large)*

stockpot

Measurement

measuring spoons

measuring cups

Tools

meat tenderizer

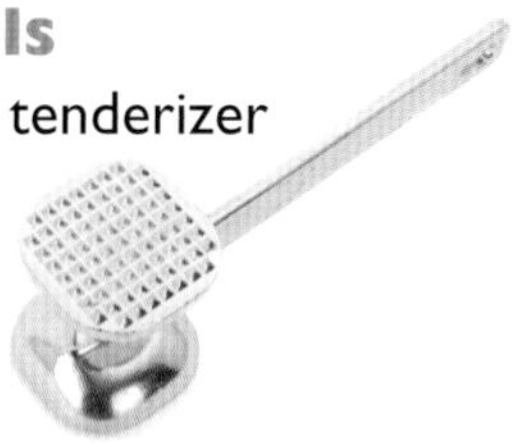

flat spatula

whisk

paring knife

chef's knife

wire cheese slicer

can opener

Other

flat-bottomed bowls *(3 medium)*

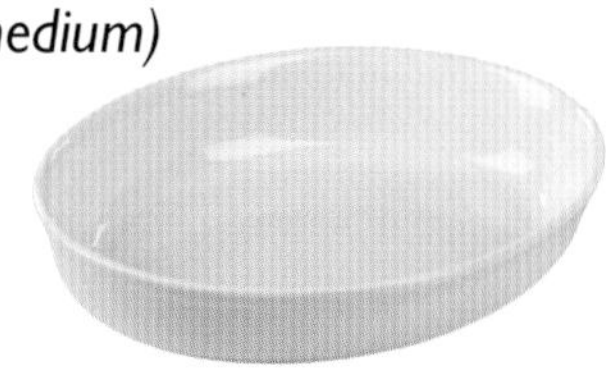

bowls *(1 medium, 2 small)*

cutting board(s)

colander

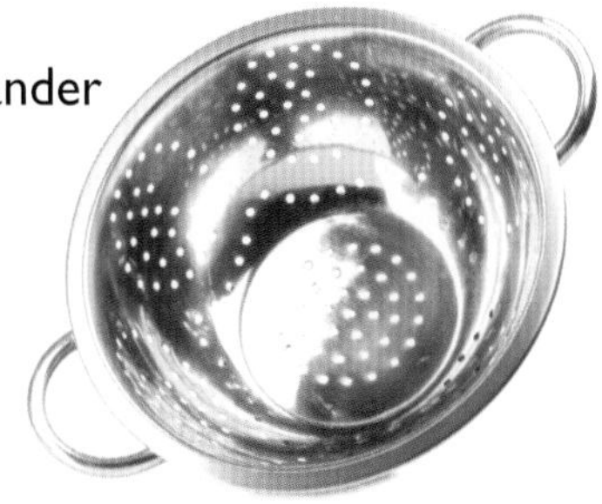

bench scraper

plates or trays *(2 large)*

foil

plastic wrap

catch-all

Click CONTINUE when you're done!

Get Set!

Watch the *Get Set!* segment before completing these steps.

- slice squash into $^1/_8$-inch slices; place in medium bowl
- cut half an onion into ½-inch slices; place in small bowl
- core and dice tomato; place in another small bowl
- peel and mince 1–2 cloves garlic; place in bowl with tomatoes

1 **Prepare** the vegetables.

- using wire cheese slicer, cut 12–15 slices mozzarella cheese

2 **Slice** the mozzarella cheese.

- cover chicken with plastic wrap; pound to ½-inch thick all over
- throw away plastic wrap; take all utensils used for the chicken to the sink
- wash your hands

3 **Pound** the chicken breasts.

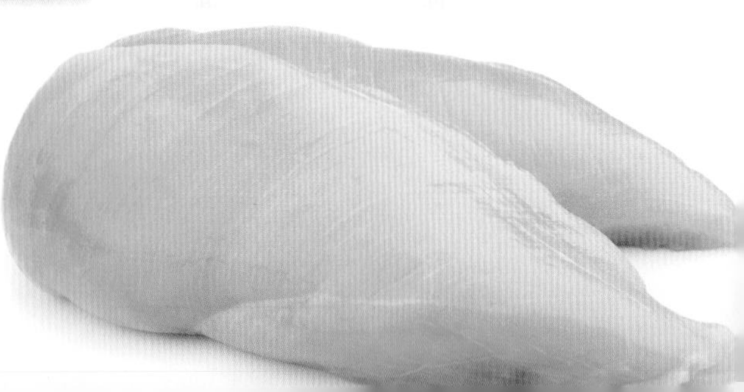

4 **Set up** the breading station.

- in one bowl, whisk together:
  - **¼ cup flour**
  - **1 tsp pepper**
  - **1 Tbsp salt**
  - **2 Tbsp Italian seasoning**
- in another bowl, whisk together:
  - **¼ cup Parmesan cheese**
  - **¼ cup breadcrumbs**
- in another bowl, whisk:
  - **3 eggs**

5 **Bread** the chicken.

- bread each chicken breast as follows:
  1. coat with flour
  2. dip into egg mixture
  3. coat with cheese and breadcrumbs

6 **Preheat** stuff.

- preheat oven to 350°F
- fill stockpot $^{2}/_{3}$ full of water
- add a **palmful of salt**
- cover stockpot and heat water over high heat

Click CONTINUE when you're done!

Get Cooking!

Watch the *Get Cooking!* segment before completing these steps.

- add fettuccini to boiling water
- set a timer according to the directions on the package

1 **Cook** the pasta.

- heat 1–2 Tbsp olive oil in large skillet on medium heat
- add chicken breasts to hot pan
- cook, undisturbed, for about 2 minutes, or until they start to brown
- flip and cook another 1–2 minutes

2 **Sauté** chicken breasts.

- arrange chicken in a greased casserole dish
- cover with marinara sauce, mozzarella cheese, and **¼ cup Parmesan cheese**
- cover with foil; poke holes to vent
- bake covered for 15 minutes; remove foil and bake uncovered another 10–15 minutes or until the cheese is bubbling and golden brown

3 **Assemble** and bake the casserole.

Make sure you take pictures as you go through the steps!

4 **Finish** preparing the pasta.

- drain cooked pasta
- return pasta to stockpot, then add:
  - a generous drizzle of olive oil
  - **½ cup Parmesan cheese**
  - salt and pepper to taste
- toss together until pasta is evenly coated
- cover stockpot; let pasta rest

5 **Sauté** the vegetables.

- heat **1–2 Tbsp olive oil** on medium-high heat
- add onions; cook until they soften and turn clear
- add zucchini and yellow squash; cook until they soften, stirring frequently
- add tomatoes, garlic, splash of balsamic vinegar *(optional)*, **1–2 tsp oregano**, and salt and pepper to taste
- cook until tomatoes are heated through

To save on clean up, use the same pan you cooked the chicken in.

6 **Plate it up and enjoy!**

- serve chicken Parmesan on top of pasta
- dish up a healthy serving of sautéed veggies
- garnish chicken and veggies with a light sprinkling of Parmesan cheese

Happy Eating!

Try making this classic "comfort food" to practice your new skills.

SERVES:
4–6

KITCHEN TIME:
30 min

READY TO SERVE:
30 min

Chicken Fried Steak

Get Ready!

Ingredients

beef round steak *(2 lb)*

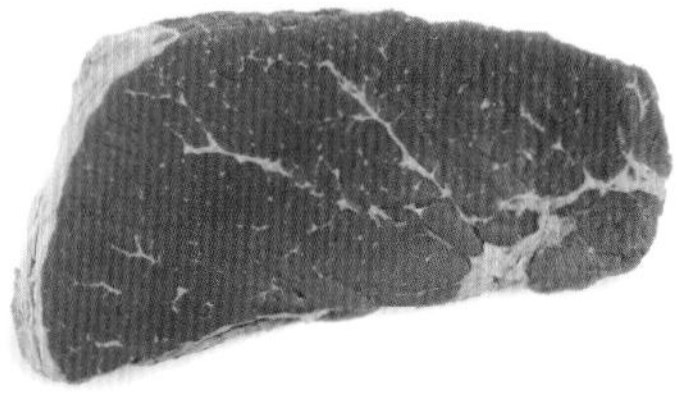

eggs *(2 large)*

flour *(1 cup)*

paprika

vegetable oil

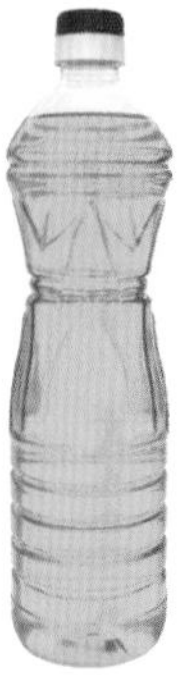

mushroom gravy mix *(1 pkg)*

OPTIONAL

green peas

instant mashed potatoes

Utensils

COOKWARE

sauté pan *(large stainless steel or cast iron)*
saucepan *(small)*
baking tray

TOOLS

meat tenderizer
tongs
whisk

MEASUREMENT

measuring spoons
measuring cups
liquid measuring cup

OTHER

flat-bottomed bowls *(2 medium)*
cutting board

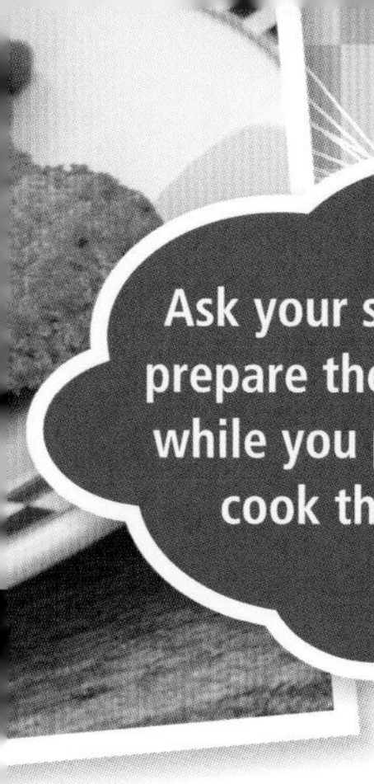

Ask your sous chef to prepare the side dishes while you prepare and cook the steaks.

STACK UP YOUR KNOWLEDGE

Don't forget to check off the STACK items you mastered on page 142.

Get Set!

1 Set up the breading station.

- into one flat-bottomed bowl, whisk together:
  - 1 cup flour
  - 1 tsp paprika
  - 1 Tbsp salt
  - 1 tsp pepper
- into another flat-bottomed bowl, whisk 2 eggs

2 Bread the steak.

- cut steak into 4 pieces
- season each piece with salt and pepper
- dredge steak pieces in flour
- using coarse side of meat tenderizer, pound beef to ¼-inch thick all over
- dip in the egg mixture
- dredge through flour again
- allow coated beef to sit for 5–10 minutes

3 Prepare gravy ingredients.

- measure ingredients according to directions on package

Get Cooking!

1 Pan-fry the steak.

- heat ¼ cup vegetable oil in large skillet over medium-high heat
- pan-fry the steak a few pieces at a time being careful not to overcrowd the pan
- cook about 4 minutes per side or until golden brown
- remove cooked steak to baking tray; cover with foil to keep warm
- repeat until all steak pieces are cooked

2 Make the gravy.

- prepare gravy according to directions on package

3 Plate it up and enjoy!

- top steaks with gravy
- plate it up with peas and mashed potatoes

Reward Yourself!

Pistachio Nut Cake

This cake is super simple to make and impossible to resist. Enjoy it plain or topped with frozen non-fat yogurt and fresh berries. Either way, you've got yourself a delicious, crowd-pleasing dessert delight!

What You'll Need

- 1 box yellow cake mix
- 2 packages Pistachio Instant Pudding Mix *(small)*
- 4 eggs
- $\frac{1}{2}$ cup vegetable oil
- $\frac{1}{3}$ cup cream
- 1 tsp mint extract
- 1 cup sour cream
- $\frac{3}{4}$ cup chocolate chips
- powdered sugar

What You'll Do

1. Mix everything except powdered sugar in a medium bowl.
2. Pour into greased Bundt cake pan.
3. Bake at 350°F for 50 minutes or until knife inserted in middle comes out clean.
4. Let cool completely, then turn onto plate.
5. Dust with powdered sugar.

See *Get Cooking! Step 6* on page 11 to review how to apply a light dusting of powdered sugar.

Expand Your Horizons!

Practice everything you've learned so far by making one or all of these delicious recipes!

Crispy Garlic Chicken Cutlets
Savory Turkey Cutlets
Eggplant Parmesan
Coconut Shrimp
Golden Fish Filets
Beef Stroganoff
Fried Zucchini
Roasted Breaded Cauliflower
Crispy Rice Cereal Squares
Banana Bread

The recipes above, and many more, are available for download at

www.yourkidscooking.net

Tell a Friend!

Invite some friends over for a cooking party. Ask each person to bring a recipe and ingredients for one course and work together to cook up an entire meal! And don't forget to take lots of pictures to share with friends and family.

LESSON 9

Pork Chops

SERVES: 4

COMPLETE THE LESSON: 40 min

READY TO SERVE: 40 min

The Magic of Pan Sauce

How do you take a plain piece of meat and turn it into a mouth-watering meal? You guessed it—with a simple pan sauce! Restaurant chefs use this "magic trick" all the time, and now you can too. Following just a few simple steps you'll be able to make all the same sauces that fancy restaurants serve, turning ordinary food into extraordinary "cuisine"—just like magic!

Get Prepared!

Here's a little Sneak Peek of how this recipe is made.

Note to the Chef

Are you ready to learn a little "kitchen magic?" That's what many chefs call a pan sauce, and for good reason. With a pan sauce, you can turn an otherwise boring meal into something really special—and in just four simple steps that take less than 10 minutes to complete. So grab your chef hats and let's cook up some magic!

1 **Pan-fry** the pork chops.

2 **Make** a pan sauce with apples and shallots.

STACK UP YOUR KNOWLEDGE

Here's what you'll learn in this lesson.

SKILLS

- ☐ core and slice apples
- ☐ make a pan sauce

TERMS

- ☐ deglazing
- ☐ fond
- ☐ caramelization
- ☐ shallot

A

3 **Boil** potatoes.

4 **Plate it up and enjoy!**

Note to the Sous Chef

The focus of this recipe is on making a pan sauce, which is a surprisingly quick and simple four-step process. The most critical step is the first step, which is pan-frying the pork chops. The key is to make sure the pan is hot—but not too hot—before adding the meat, and then just letting it cook, undisturbed, until it lifts easily from the pan. If you can make yourself available to oversee this step in the process, it's smooth sailing the rest of the way.

COOKING KNOW-HOW

- ☐ making a pan sauce
- ☐ boiling potatoes
- ☐ how to tell the doneness of meat

Get Prepared!

When you're ready to start cooking, watch ***Recipe 9: Pork Chops.***

What You'll Need

. . . to make Pork Chops

Shopping List

- pork chops (4 1-inch thick)
- red potatoes (6 medium)
- apple (1 large)
- shallot (1 large)
- parsley (1 bunch)
- butter (1 stick)
- cream (1/4 cup)
- chicken bouillon (1 cube or 1 Tbsp)
- olive oil
- cumin
- sage
- thyme

An Easy-Fix Option for this recipe can be downloaded for free at

www.yourkidscooking.net

. . . and to Complete Your Meal

carrots | cauliflower | broccoli

To make half your plate fruits and vegetables, we recommend serving this meal with a medley of fresh steamed carrots, broccoli, and cauliflower.

Shopping Tip

There are 2 common cuts of pork chops—loin chops and sirloin chops. The loin chops are leaner and have less fat and the meat is lighter in color. The sirloin chops are a little darker in color and have more fat distributed throughout the meat, making them much more moist and tender. For this recipe, thick-sliced chops of either type will work better than thin-sliced chops.

Visit www.yourkidscooking.net to learn more!

What's On Your Plate?

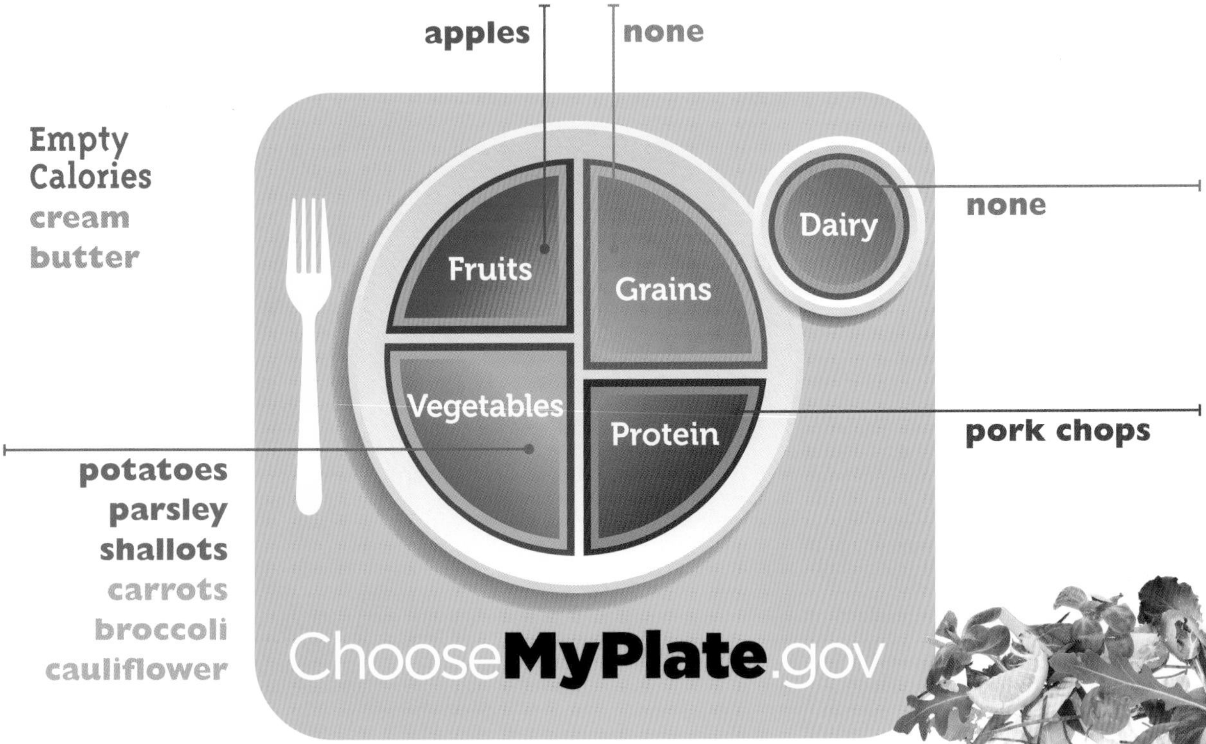

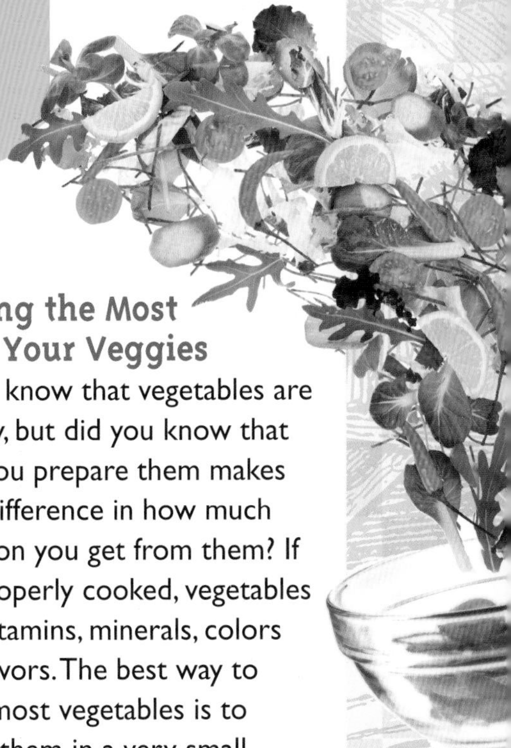

In the Spotlight

Pork can be a fairly lean source of quality protein. The leanest cuts are tenderloin, loin chops and sirloin roast. These leaner cuts are high in protein, low in fat and have more B-vitamins than many other types of meat. Bacon is high in saturated fat and cholesterol and ham falls somewhere in the middle.

Potatoes, when cooked and eaten properly, are very good for you. Not only are they a great source of carbohydrates (your body's primary source of fuel), they are also a good source of vitamin C, potassium, and fiber—especially if you eat the skin. They are a healthy and low-fat food when baked or boiled and eaten without lots of high-fat toppings like butter, sour cream, or gravy.

Getting the Most from Your Veggies

We all know that vegetables are healthy, but did you know that how you prepare them makes a big difference in how much nutrition you get from them? If not properly cooked, vegetables lose vitamins, minerals, colors and flavors. The best way to cook most vegetables is to steam them in a very small amount of water. Make sure that the water is hot to start with, so that the vegetables are in the steamer as little as possible. The more water you can keep in your vegetables, the more nutrients they will retain. For the best nutrition, steam them until they're crisp-tender.

Get Ready!

Start *Recipe 9: Pork Chops* before completing this step.

Ingredients

pork chops *(4)*

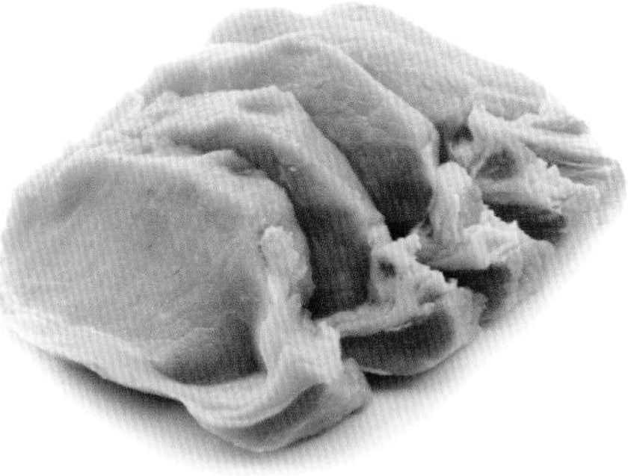

red potatoes *(6)*

apple *(1)*

shallot *(1)*

parsley *(1 bunch)*

butter *(1 stick)*

cream

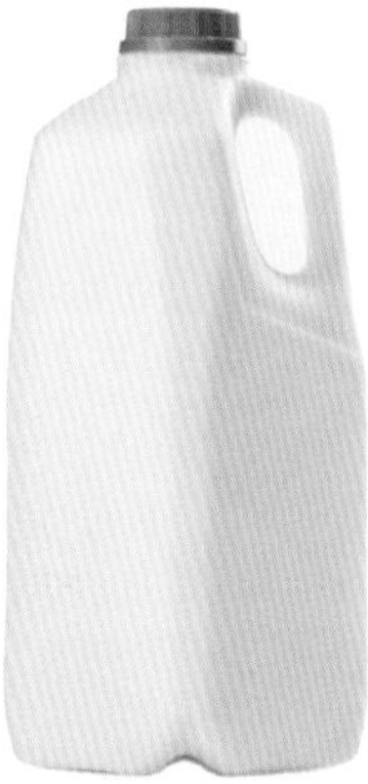

chicken bouillon

olive oil

cumin

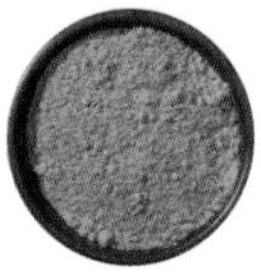

sage

thyme

Complete Your Meal

carrots | broccoli | cauliflower

Utensils

Cookware

stockpot *(or large saucepan)*

sauté pan *(large, stainless steel)*

baking dish or serving platter

Measurement

liquid measuring cup

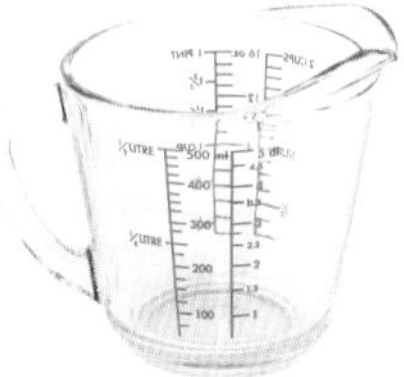

measuring spoons

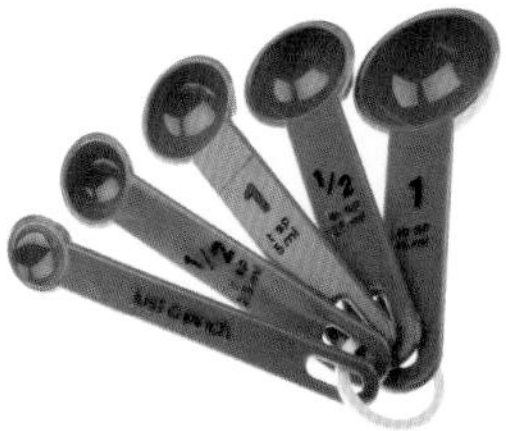

Tools

chef's knife

paring knife

tongs or large fork

flat spatula

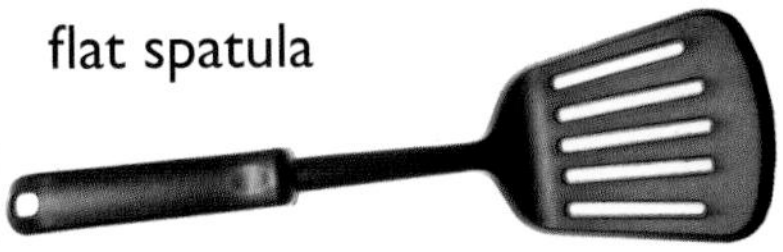

wooden spoon

Other

bowls *(3 small, 1 medium)*

colander

cutting board(s)

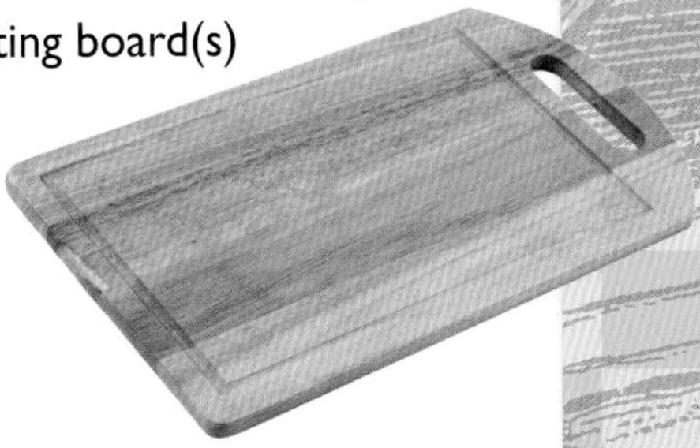

bench scraper

catch-all

Click CONTINUE when you're done!

Get Set!

Watch the *Get Set!* segment before completing these steps.

- slice shallot into thin slices about 1/8-inch thick
- transfer shallots to small bowl

1 **Peel and slice** the shallots.

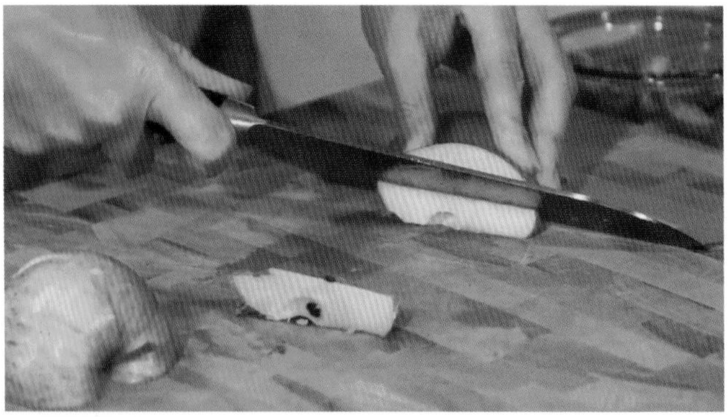

- cut apple into quarters
- cut core and stem from each quarter
- cut each quarter into 1/8-inch slices
- transfer apple slices to medium bowl

2 **Core and slice** the apple.

- cut potatoes into large bite-size pieces
- place in stockpot; cover in 2–3 inches water
- heat water over medium-high heat

3 **Cut** up the potatoes.

- mince $^{1}/_{3}$ **cup parsley**
- transfer to small bowl

4 Mince the parsley.

- measure **1 cup hot water** into a liquid measuring cup
- add **1 tsp chicken bouillon granules** or **1 bouillon cube**; stir until completely dissolved

5 Make the chicken broth.

Complete Your Meal

Ask your sous chef to prepare the steamed vegetables while you complete steps 5 and 6.

- in small bowl, combine:
  - **1 tsp salt**
  - **¼ tsp pepper**
  - **1 tsp thyme**
  - **1 tsp cumin**
  - **1 tsp sage**
- apply spice rub to pork chops
- wash your hands

6 Apply rub to pork chops.

Click CONTINUE when you're done!

Get Cooking!

Watch the *Get Cooking!* segment before completing these steps.

- heat **2 Tbsp oil** over medium heat
- add pork chops to hot pan; allow to cook, undisturbed, until edges turn white about halfway up the sides
- flip pork chops and cook to desired doneness

1 Pan-fry the pork chops.

See *Get Cooking! Step 1* on the DVD to review how to tell the doneness of meat.

Keep an eye on the potatoes while you cook the pork chops.

- add shallots and apples to hot pan
- cook until shallots turn soft and apples begin to release their juices
- slowly add chicken broth, adjusting heat to maintain a simmer
- cook until broth is reduced by about half, deglazing the pan with your spatula while it simmers
- add **1 Tbsp butter** and **¼ cup cream**

2 Make the pan sauce.

Cut remaining butter into small chunks to be added to the potatoes later on.

- season with **salt and pepper** to taste
- continue to simmer until sauce cooks down and starts to thicken
- pour sauce over pork chops and loosely cover with foil

Make sure you take pictures as you go through the steps!

- when potatoes are "fork tender," drain in a colander
- return to stockpot; add parsley, remaining butter and salt and pepper to taste
- stir gently with a wooden spoon until butter is melted and potatoes are evenly coated with butter and parsley

3 Make the parsley potatoes.

- to serve "family style" put everything on the table in nice serving dishes and let everyone help themselves

4 Plate it up and enjoy!

Happy Eating!

Test Your Skills!

Try making this light and delicious recipe to practice your new skills.

SERVES:
4

KITCHEN TIME:
30 min

READY TO SERVE:
30 min

Chicken Picatta with Parsley Pasta

Get Ready!

Ingredients

chicken breasts
(*2 boneless, skinless*)

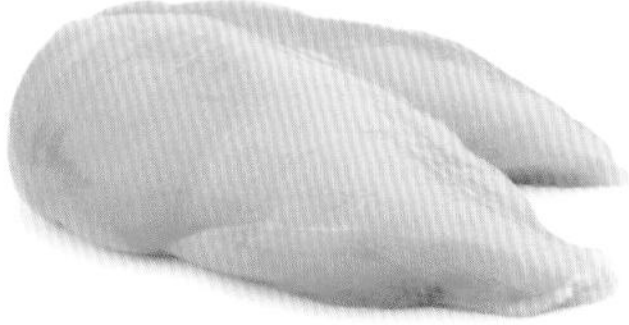

linguine (*1 lb*)

flour (*¼ cup*)

butter (*6 Tbsp*)

olive oil

lemons (*3 large or ¼ cup juice*)

chicken stock or broth (*½ cup*)

capers (*¼ cup brined*)

parsley (*1 bunch*)

OPTIONAL

green salad

Utensils

COOKWARE

sauté pan
(*large, stainless steel*)
stockpot

TOOLS

chef's knife
meat tenderizer
flat spatula
whisk
colander
cutting board
catch-all

MEASUREMENT

liquid measuring cup
measuring cups

OTHER

flat-bottomed bowl
bowls (*3 small*)

STACK UP YOUR KNOWLEDGE Don't forget to check off the STACK items you mastered on page 142.

Get Set!

1 Prepare chicken breasts.

- measure ¼ cup flour into flat-bottomed bowl
- use meat tenderizer to flatten chicken breasts to ¼-inch thick
- season both sides with salt and pepper to taste
- coat both sides of flattened chicken breasts with thin layer of flour

2 Prepare ingredients for pan sauce.

- measure ¼ cup lemon juice into small bowl
- measure ¼ cup capers into another small bowl
- measure ½ cup chicken stock into liquid measuring cup
- chop ½ cup parsley; place in small bowl

3 Prepare water for pasta.

- fill stockpot ¾ full of water
- add palmful of salt
- heat over high-heat

Get Cooking!

1 Cook the pasta.

- add linguine to boiling water
- cook according to directions on package

2 Pan-fry the chicken breasts.

- heat 2 Tbsp olive oil in sauté pan over medium heat
- add chicken breasts to hot pan
- cook chicken for 2–3 minutes, or until golden brown
- flip chicken and cook on other side until golden brown
- remove to platter; cover with foil to keep warm

3 Make pan sauce.

- increase heat to medium high
- add ½ cup chicken stock, ¼ cup lemon juice, and ¼ cup capers
- simmer liquid 4–5 minutes or until reduced by about half, scraping up fond as it cooks
- stir 2 Tbsp butter and ¼ cup parsley into sauce; cook over low heat until sauce thickens slightly
- pour thickened pan sauce over chicken

4 Finish the parsley pasta.

- toss ¼ cup parsley and 4 Tbsp butter into pasta until evenly coated

5 Plate it up and enjoy!

- serve chicken and pasta with a green salad
- garnish each plate with lemon slices

Reward Yourself!

Try substituting your favorite berry, or a combination of berries, for one cup of apples.

Apple Crisp

This is the best recipe if you're looking for an old-fashioned, delicious apple dessert that's quick and easy to make. Using a variety of fresh apples, and the perfect blend of spices, this apple crisp promises a true delight in every forkful.

What You'll Need

- 4–6 apples (4 cups)
- ¾ cup packed brown sugar
- ½ cup all-purpose flour
- ½ cup quick-cooking or old-fashioned oats
- ½ cup chopped walnuts
- ⅓ cup butter or margarine, softened
- ½ tsp cinnamon
- ½ tsp nutmeg

What You'll Do

1. Heat oven to 375°F. Grease bottom and sides of 9-inch square baking dish with shortening or cooking spray.
2. Core and slice apples; cut into bite-size pieces; spread in baking dish.
3. Combine remaining ingredients in a medium bowl; stir until well mixed; sprinkle over apples.
4. Bake 25–30 minutes or until topping is golden brown and apples are fork tender.

Expand your Horizons!

Practice everything you've learned so far by making one or all of these delicious recipes.

Rye-Crusted Pork Schnitzel
Filet of Sole Almondine
Biscuits with Sausage Gravy
Pork Tenderloins with Marsala Sauce
Lemon Chicken
Salisbury Steak with Mushroom Sauce
Potato Salad
Waldorf Salad
Apple Pie
Applesauce

The recipes above, and many more, are available for download at

www.yourkidscooking.net

Tell a Friend!

Together with your sous chef, start a recipe exchange with all your social media friends. Share recipes and pictures of some of your favorite dishes and invite friends to share their favorites as well. Try making a few that sound particularly good to you.

LESSON 10

Pot Roast

SERVES: 4–6

COMPLETE THE LESSON: 30 min

READY TO SERVE: 5–6 hours

Pot Roast: An All-American Meal

Pot roast, as it's commonly called today, evolved from the colonial-era New England "boiled dinner." During the 1700's it became known as Yankee Pot Roast. You will be making what is commonly referred to as "Cowboy" Pot Roast, which is simply the wild, wild west's version of its Yankee cousin. Either way, pot roast is easy to make, delicious to eat, and a truly all-American meal.

Get Prepared!

Here's a little Sneak Peek of how this recipe is made.

Note to the Chef
You're going to complete your repertoire of cooking skills by learning about the slow-cooking method of preparing food. Basically you just put whatever you want in one pot—meat, chicken, fish, vegetables, even fruit—add some liquid, and then just let it cook over very low heat for several hours. It's super easy and super good. You can make it early in the day, go out and have some fun, and when you come back, it's supper time!

1 **Sear** the chuck roast.

2 **Slow-cook** roast for 4–6 hours.

STACK UP YOUR KNOWLEDGE

Here's what you'll learn in this lesson.

SKILLS
- ☐ mash potatoes
- ☐ sear meat

TERMS
- ☐ sear
- ☐ slow-cooking

A

3 **Boil** and **mash** potatoes.

4 **Plate it up and enjoy!**

Note to the Sous Chef

The focus of this lesson is on learning about the slow-cooking method of preparing food. Pot roast is cooked very slowly over low heat for several hours, making it a great make-ahead meal. It's served with mashed potatoes, which can be made after the roast is done and resting in the Dutch oven. In the meantime, there's not much for the sous chef to do—except maybe enjoy a little extra quality time with the chef!

COOKING KNOW-HOW

- ☐ searing meat
- ☐ slow-cooking

When you're ready to start cooking, watch *Recipe 10: Pot Roast.*

What You'll Need

. . . to make Pot Roast

Shopping List

- chuck roast (3–4 lb)
- carrots (1–2 large)
- celery (1 stalk)
- garlic (1–3 cloves)
- onion (1 medium)
- potatoes (4–6 medium)
- milk (1 cup)
- diced tomatoes (1 15-oz can)
- apple juice, beef broth or cooking sherry (1/2 cup)
- butter (1 stick)
- sage
- thyme
- rosemary

. . . and to

Complete Your Meal

green beans

Pot roast is a real "meat and potatoes" meal that provides lots of protein, but little nutrition from vegetables. Serve with green beans or other fresh vegetable of your choice to make it a more nutritionally complete meal.

Shopping Tip

Although this recipe calls for using a chuck roast, pot roast can be made with other cuts of beef as well. Because the slow-cooking method tenderizes tougher, and consequently more affordable, cuts of beef, you can choose from several types of roasts, including blade, cross rib, top blade, bottom blade boneless, brisket and shoulder. When in doubt, ask the butcher for recommendations.

An Easy-Fix Option for this recipe can be downloaded for free at

www.yourkidscooking.net

What's On Your Plate?

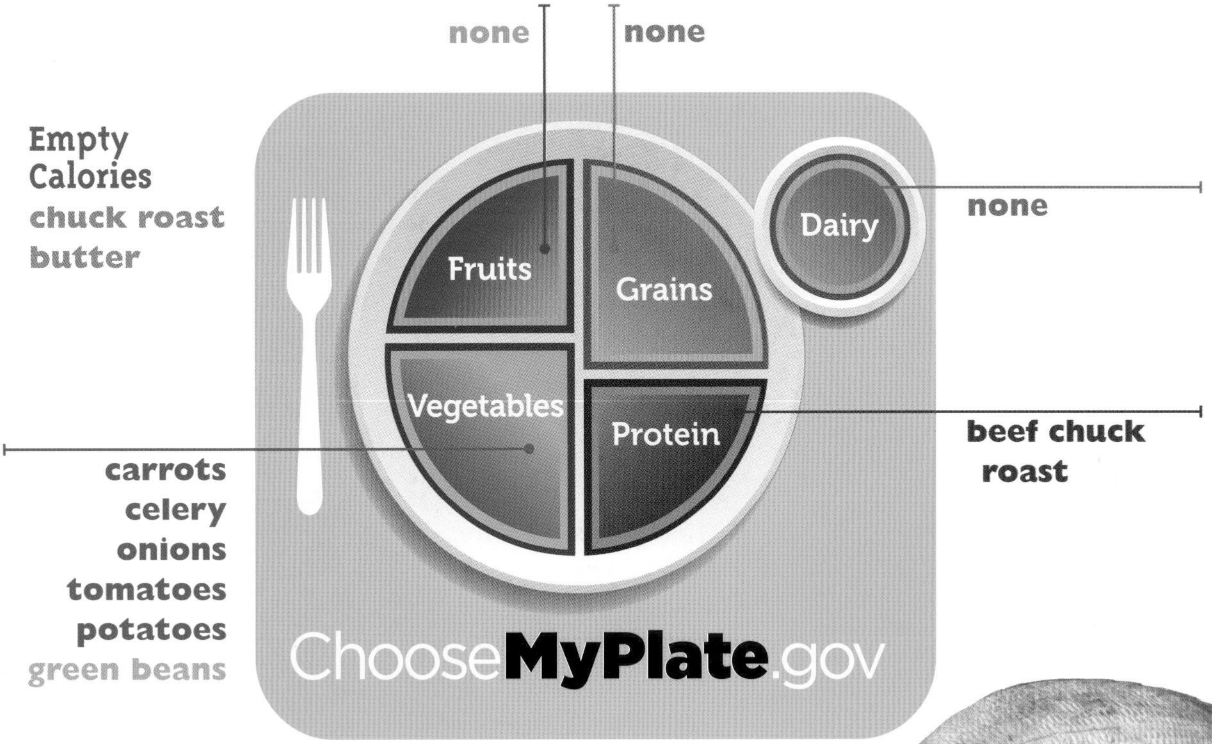

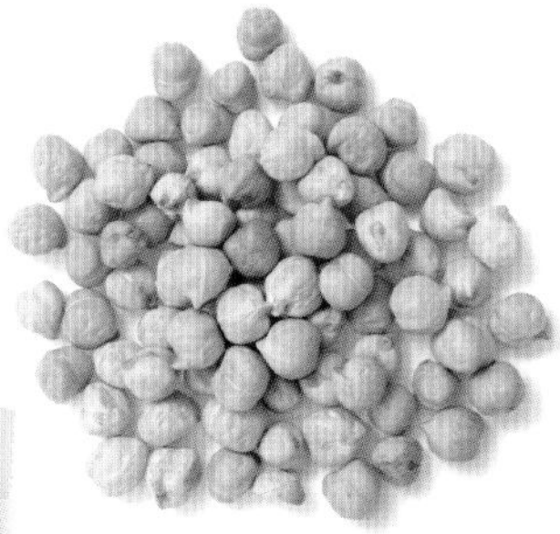

Chuck roast contains more fat than some roasts, but also more flavor. When the roast is slow-cooked in liquid, as in this recipe, much of the fat is cooked off and ends up in the liquid. To remove the fat, allow the liquid to cool. The fat will harden on the top of the liquid making it easy to scoop out with a spoon.

The Many Sources of Proteins

Eat a variety of foods from the protein group each week. Experiment with main dishes made with beans or legumes, poultry, and soy. Eat seafood in place of meat or poultry twice a week. Choose lean or low-fat protein sources such as chicken, pork, and extra-lean ground beef. Trim or drain fat from meat and remove poultry skin to reduce fat and calories.

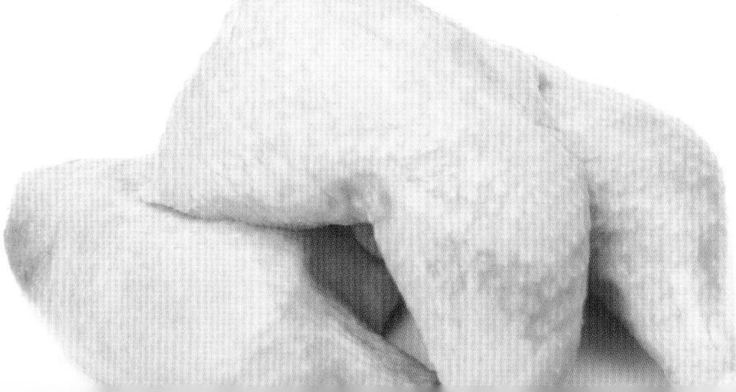

Get Ready!

Start *Recipe 10: Pot Roast* before completing this step.

Ingredients

chuck roast

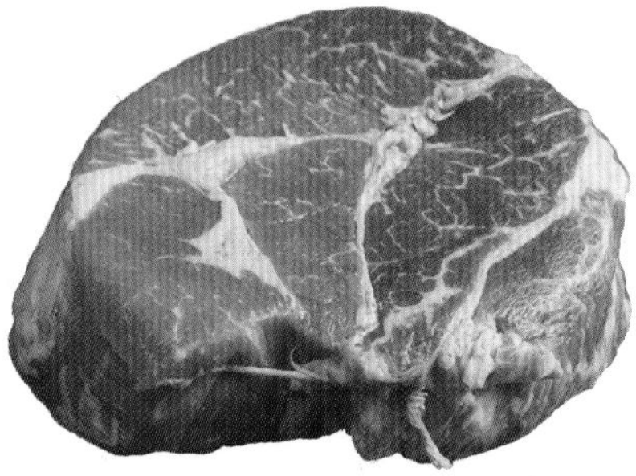

carrots *(2)*

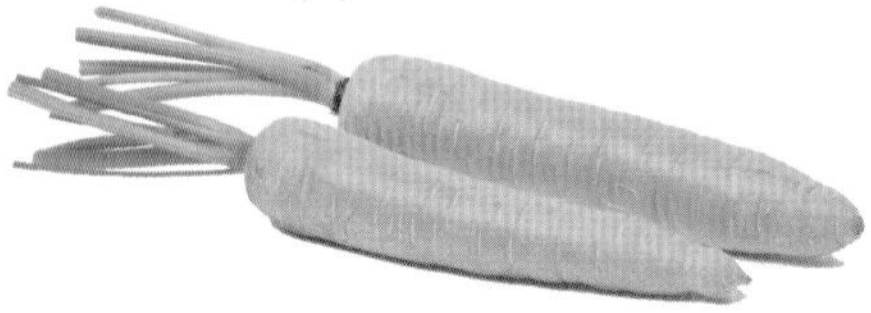

celery *(1 stalk)*

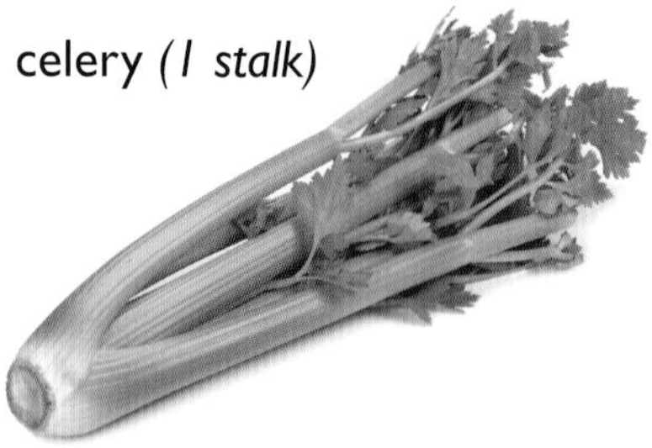

garlic *(1–3 cloves)*

onion *(1)*

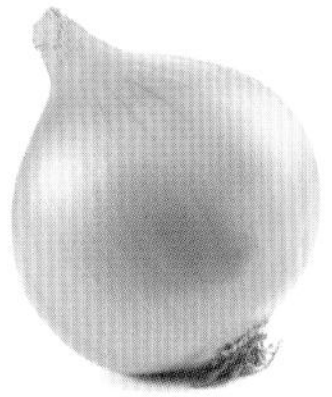

potatoes *(4–6 medium)*

diced tomatoes *(1 15-oz can)*

apple juice, beef broth or cooking sherry *(½ cup)*

butter *(1 stick)*

sage

thyme

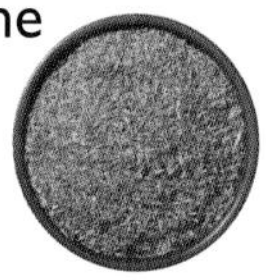

rosemary

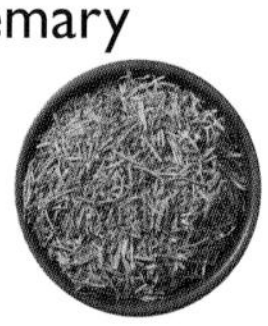

Complete Your Meal

green beans

Preparing meals using the one-pot, slow-cooking method was one of the few options available to cowboys living out on the open range. Today we use it mostly because it's a super easy way to make a super delicious meal!

Utensils

Cookware

Dutch oven

stockpot

Measurement

liquid measuring cup

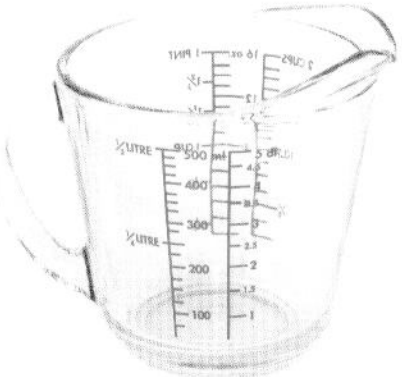

measuring spoons

Tools

chef's knife

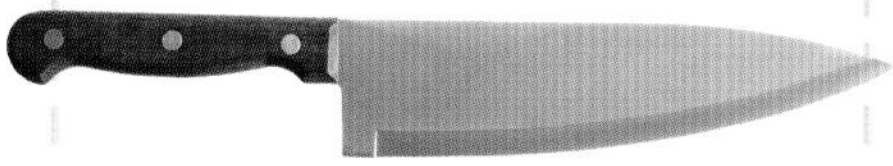

meat fork

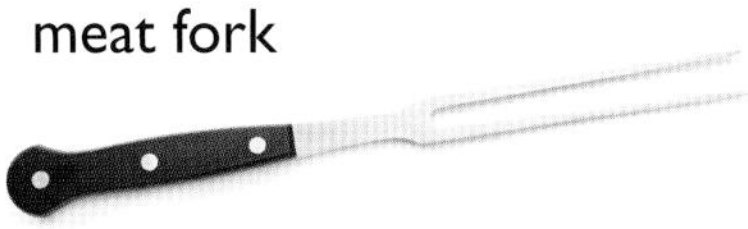

can opener

potato masher

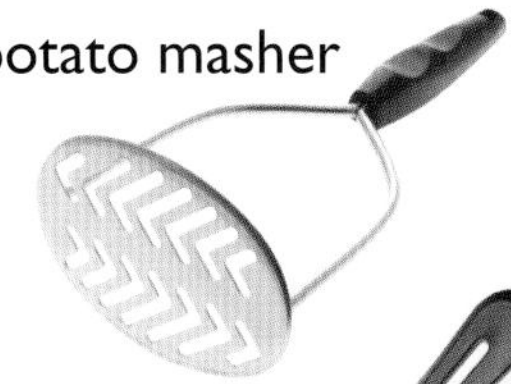

flat spatula

vegetable peeler

Other

cutting board(s)

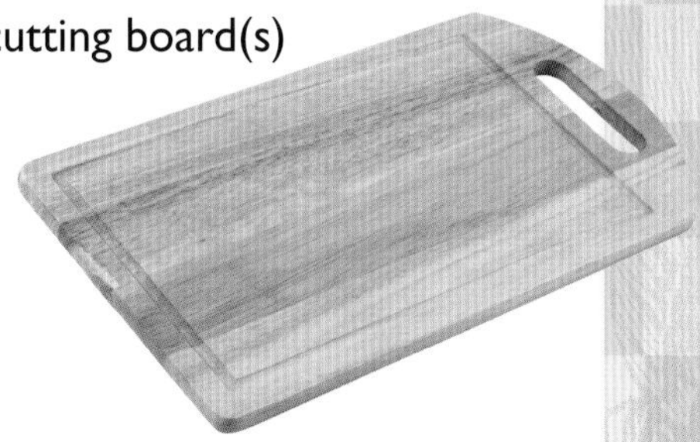

bowl *(2 small, 1 medium)*

foil

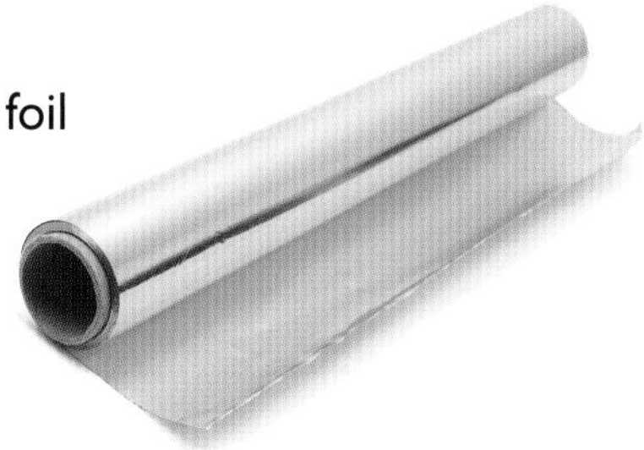

colander

Click CONTINUE when you're done!

Get Set!

Watch the *Get Set!* segment before completing these steps.

- into medium bowl, place:
  - sliced carrots
  - sliced celery
  - diced onion
- mince garlic; transfer to small bowl
- open diced tomatoes; do not drain

1 Prepare the vegetables.

- in a small bowl, combine:
  - **½ tsp pepper**
  - **1 tsp salt**
  - **1 tsp sage**
  - **1 tsp thyme**
  - **1 tsp rosemary**
- apply spice rub all over the roast
- wash your hands

2 Prepare the roast.

Make sure you take pictures as you go through the steps!

Wait to complete step 3 until about a half hour before the roast is done.

3 **Prepare** mashed potato ingredients.

- cut potatoes into 8 pieces each
- place in stockpot; cover with 2–3 inches of water
- cut **6 Tbsp butter** into small chunks
- measure **1 cup milk** into a liquid measuring cup

Guess What!

Some say the recipe for mashed potatoes originated in 1771 when a French man named Antoine Parmentier came up with the idea of having a competition on ways to make potatoes. Since it was his idea, it's no surprise that his recipe for mashed potatoes won first place. Soon after, mashed potatoes were introduced into the cuisine of France, and eventually, the rest of Europe.

Click **CONTINUE** when you're done!

Get Cooking!

Watch the *Get Cooking!* segment before completing these steps.

- heat **2–3 Tbsp oil** in Dutch oven
- sear roast on all sides (1–2 minutes on each side)
- use meat fork and spatula to remove roast to large platter

1 Sear the roast.

- heat another **1 Tbsp oil** in Dutch oven
- cook carrots, celery, and onion over medium heat until they begin to release their moisture and onions turn clear
- add garlic and cook another 1–2 minutes or until garlic softens a bit

2 Sauté the vegetables.

- add ½ **cup liquid** (apple juice, beef broth or sherry) to Dutch oven
- return roast to Dutch oven
- pour canned tomatoes over roast
- cook, covered, over lowest heat setting for 4–5 hours

3 Slow-cook the roast.

Make sure you take pictures as you go through the steps!

Wait to complete step 4 until about 20 minutes before the roast is done.

4 **Make** the mashed potatoes.

- boil the potatoes for about 20 minutes or until they are fork tender; drain in colander
- return to stockpot and add:
  - **butter pieces**
  - **1Tbsp salt**
  - **pinch of pepper**
  - **½ cup or so of milk**
- mash potatoes, adding milk as needed to reach desired consistency
- cover to keep warm

5 **Finish** the roast.

- transfer cooked roast to serving platter using meat fork and spatula
- cover roast with foil tent
- let roast rest for 15–20 minutes before serving
- simmer liquid in the Dutch oven, uncovered, until it thickens up a bit

Complete Your Meal

Ask your sous chef to prepare the green beans while the roast is resting.

6 **Plate it up and enjoy!**

- cut or break roast apart into serving-size pieces
- cover roast with thickened liquid and pour any remaining liquid into a gravy boat or bowl
- serve family style

Happy Eating!

Test Your Skills!

Here's another delicious dish you can make to practice your new skills.

SERVES:
4–6

KITCHEN TIME:
30 min

READY TO SERVE:
50 min

Shepard's Pie

Get Ready!

Ingredients

ground beef or lamb *(1 ½ lb)*

onion *(1 medium)*

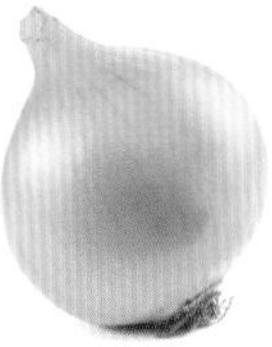

carrots *(2)*

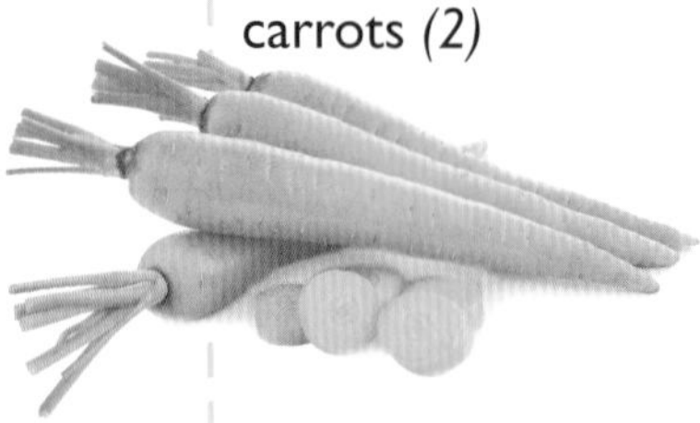

peas *(1 cup frozen)*

flour *(¼ cup)*

tomato paste *(1 Tbsp)*

chicken broth *(2 cups)*

thyme

garlic *(2 cloves)*

Worcestershire sauce *(2 tsp)*

potatoes *(4 medium)*

milk *(½ cup)*

eggs *(2 large)*

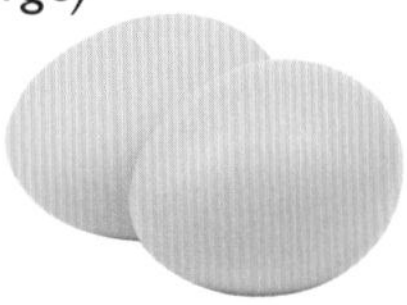

butter *(6 Tbsp)*

paprika *(optional)*

Utensils

COOKWARE
stockpot
sauté pan *(large)*
casserole dish *(10 x 10 inches)*

TOOLS
chef's knife
flat spatula
potato masher
vegetable peeler
can opener

MEASUREMENT
liquid measuring cup
measuring cups
measuring spoons

OTHER
bowls *(1 small)*
cutting board
catch-all

STACK UP YOUR KNOWLEDGE

Don't forget to check off the STACK items you mastered on page 142.

Get Set!

1 Prepare mashed potatoes ingredients.

- cut up 4 potatoes; place in stockpot; cover with 2–3 inches of water
- cut 4 Tbsp butter into small chunks
- into a medium bowl, whisk together:
  - 2 egg yolks
  - ½ cup milk

2 Prepare veggies for filling.

- peel and dice 2 carrots
- peel and dice 1 onion
- measure 1 cup frozen peas into measuring cup

3 Measure ingredients for gravy.

- measure ¼ cup flour into small bowl
- into a liquid measuring cup, combine:
  - 2 cups chicken broth
  - 2 tsp Worcestershire sauce
  - 1 tsp thyme

Get Cooking!

400° Pre-heat

1 Make mashed potatoes.

- cook and drain potatoes
- return to stockpot; add butter, egg yolks and milk
- mash the potatoes, adding more milk as needed

2 Brown the ground meat.

In the large sauté pan:

- brown the ground beef or lamb
- drain meat into colander

3 Cook the veggies.

In the same pan, melt 2 Tbsp butter, then:

- cook carrots and onions 5–7 minutes until softened
- add garlic; cook 1–2 minutes
- stir in ¼ cup flour and 1 Tbsp tomato paste; cook, stirring constantly until flour is incorporated, about 1 minute
- slowly stir in broth mixture; bring to a simmer, scraping up fond
- reduce heat to medium-low; cook until sauce has thickened, about 3–5 minutes

4 Finish cooking the filling.

- turn off heat; stir in drained meat and peas
- season with salt and pepper to taste

5 Assemble and bake the pie.

- fill casserole dish with meat filling
- spread potatoes evenly over casserole
- dust potatoes with 1 tsp sweet paprika
- bake until top is golden brown, about 20 minutes

6 Plate it up and enjoy!

- plate it up with a crisp green salad

Reward Yourself!

Pineapple Upside Down Cake

An old-fashioned classic, this crowd pleaser is easy enough to make on a busy weeknight yet elegant enough for a special occasion. Either way, this recipe turns an ordinary cake into an extraordinarily delicious dessert!

What You'll Need

- 1 box yellow cake mix
- ¼ cup *(½ stick)* butter
- 1 cup firmly-packed brown sugar
- 1 *(20 oz)* can pineapple slices
- Maraschino cherries

Check the cake mix box for other ingredients you may need to make the cake.

What You'll Do

1. Prepare cake mix according to directions on the box.
2. Melt butter in small sauce pan.
3. Pour butter evenly into a 9-inch cake pan.
4. Sprinkle the brown sugar evenly over the butter.
5. Arrange the pineapple slices on top of brown sugar; place one cherry in the center of each pineapple slice.
6. Pour batter evenly over fruit; bake according to directions on package.

Expand Your Horizons!

Practice everything you've learned so far by making one or all of these delicious recipes.

Hunter's Stew
Chicken and Dumplings
Chicken Cacciatore
Corned Beef and Cabbage
Chili Verde
Arroz con Pollo
Irish Stew
Minestrone Soup
Split Pea Soup
Strawberry-Rhubarb Pie

The recipes above, and many more, are available for download at

www.yourkidscooking.net

Tell a Friend!

Ask your sous chef to help you start a blog and share your knowledge and enthusiasm for cooking with the world! Let everyone know how fun and easy it can be to make wholesome and delicious food. You may be surprised at how many people you can inspire by sharing your experience.

Reflections

STACK

UP YOUR KNOWLEDGE

Use the chart to the right to track your progress. Check off the STACK items you master in each recipe-lesson. When you've got all the items checked off go to **www.YourKidsCooking.net** to request your personalized Young Chef's Certificate of Completion.

SKILLS

- ☐ bread chicken
- ☐ brown ground beef
- ☐ chop herbs
- ☐ chop onions
- ☐ core and slice apples
- ☐ core tomatoes
- ☐ crack eggs
- ☐ flip food with a spatula
- ☐ grate cheese
- ☐ make a pan sauce
- ☐ mash potatoes
- ☐ measure dry ingredients
- ☐ measure liquids
- ☐ open cans
- ☐ peel and mince garlic
- ☐ peel vegetables
- ☐ poach eggs
- ☐ pound chicken
- ☐ prepare peapods
- ☐ roll out a pie crust
- ☐ sear meat
- ☐ separate eggs
- ☐ shape meatballs
- ☐ slice celery
- ☐ slice cheese
- ☐ slice peppers
- ☐ use a knife safely
- ☐ use a pastry blender
- ☐ use measuring spoons
- ☐ whisk eggs

TERMS AND

- ☐ bench scraper
- ☐ breading
- ☐ brown
- ☐ caramelization
- ☐ chop
- ☐ colander
- ☐ cutting in
- ☐ deglazing
- ☐ dice
- ☐ double-boiler
- ☐ dust
- ☐ flat spatula
- ☐ fond
- ☐ full boil
- ☐ mince
- ☐ pastry blender
- ☐ poach
- ☐ rolling pin
- ☐ roux
- ☐ rubber spatula
- ☐ sauté
- ☐ sear
- ☐ separate eggs

- □ shallot
- □ simmer
- □ slow boil
- □ slow-cooking
- □ slurry
- □ stir-fry
- □ vegetable peeler
- □ whisk
- □ wok

Cooking Know-How

- □ baking casseroles
- □ best oils for stir-frying
- □ boiling potatoes
- □ boiling rice
- □ browning meat
- □ Chinese spices
- □ cooking bacon
- □ cooking garlic
- □ cooking onions
- □ cooking pasta
- □ cooking spinach
- □ cooking with butter
- □ cooking with oil
- □ how to make a cheese sauce
- □ how to tell the doneness of meat
- □ kitchen safety (draining pasta)
- □ kitchen safety (handling raw meat)
- □ kitchen safety (using a knife)
- □ making a pan sauce
- □ making Hollandaise sauce
- □ making pie crust
- □ pan-frying
- □ poaching eggs
- □ preheating pans
- □ sautéing vegetables
- □ searing meat
- □ slow-cooking
- □ stir-frying basics
- □ testing for doneness
- □ thickening sauces
- □ timing it right
- □ tomato-based sauces
- □ using a double-boiler

My Cooking Journal

Use these pages to reflect on your cooking experience!

Your Kids: Cooking!

My Cooking Journal

Use these pages to reflect on your cooking experience!